I0486596

This book was written in
33 lifetimes and 90 minutes.

We do not have to understand new things but by dint of patience, effort and method to come to understand with our whole self the truths which are evident.
—Simone Weil, 1952

The question is whether thinking and other invisible and soundless mental activities are meant to appear or whether in fact they can never find an adequate home in the world.
—Hannah Arendt, 1971

I believe that any communication is by nature pedagogical—one tries to persuade one way or another—so I don't see any particular difference between what is considered art and what is considered classroom activity...all activities should be creative and help expand knowledge. So a noncreative curator or teacher is a waste of time, and a nonpedagogical artist tends to deal with self-indulgence and self-therapy and therefore isn't very useful either.
—Luis Camnitzer, 2014

with
Kevin Allen
Maria Barreda
Jaime Carroll
Michelle Choman
Emily Courtney
Miriam Cutelis
Mackenzie Escobar
Lynn Gudhus
Melinda Hale
Jennifer Hesla
Tami E. Johnson
Jordan Kivitz
Ana Celina Knez
Joanna Lewton
Gaye Makin
Janet Mays
Mary Ruth McGinn
Jennifer Messman
Amy Oswalt
Andrea Perll
Tahmena Rauf
Adzua Robinson
Suzy Scollon
C.Renee Seay
Banafsheh Shearer
Emily Shepardson
Johab Silva
Elizabeth Snead
Hannah Topka
Lauren Tredinnick
Rebecca Winner
Anna Zwegat

TEACHER AS
ARTIST-IN-RESIDENCE
*The most radical form of
expression to ever exist*

~

Jorge Lucero

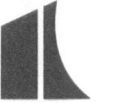

**The John F. Kennedy
Center for the
Performing Arts**

Copyright © 2020 Jorge Lucero, et al. and the Kennedy Center for the Performing Arts. This publication was made on the occasion of Jorge Lucero's participation in the 2019-2020 *Changing Education Through the Arts* programing at the John F. Kennedy Center for the Performing Arts; part of the *Rubenstein Arts Access Program*, which is generously funded by David M. Rubenstein.

Additional support is provided by Laird Norton Family Foundation, the National Committee for the Performing Arts, The Morris and Gwendolyn Cafritz Foundation, and the U.S. Department of Education.

Gifts and grants to educational programs at the Kennedy Center are provided by A. James & Alice B. Clark Foundation; Sandra K. & Clement C. Alpert; Annenberg Foundation; Bank of America; Bender Foundation, Inc.; The Honorable Stuart Bernstein and Wilma E. Bernstein; Michael F. and Noémi K. Neidorff and The Centene Charitable Foundation; CMA Foundation; Dalio Foundation; DC Commission on the Arts and Humanities; Dr. Gerald and Paula McNichols Foundation; Estée Lauder; Exelon; Ford Foundation; The Gessner Family Foundation; GRoW @ Annenberg and Gregory Annenberg Weingarten and Family; Harman Family Foundation; The Harold and Mimi Steinberg Charitable Trust; Herb Alpert Foundation; The Isadore and Bertha Gudelsky Family Foundation, Inc.; iTheatrics; The J. Willard and Alice S. Marriott Foundation; Jim and Heather Johnson; The Karel Komárek Family Foundation; the Kimsey Endowment; The Kiplinger Foundation; The King-White Family Foundation and Dr. J. Douglas White; Natalie and Herb Kohler and Kohler Co.; Laird Norton Family Foundation; Macy's; The Markow Totevy Foundation; Dr. Gary Mather and Ms. Christina Co Mather; Linda and Tobia Mercuro; Little Kids Rock; The Meredith Foundation; The Millennium Stage Endowment Fund; The Morningstar Foundation; The Morris and Gwendolyn Cafritz Foundation; Myra and Leura Younker Endowment Fund; NAMM Foundation; National Endowment for the Arts; Newman's Own Foundation; Nordstrom; Oath Founda-tion; The Orlebeke Foundation; Park Foundation, Inc.; Paul M. Angell Family Foundation; The Irene Pollin Audience Development and Community Engagement Initiatives; Prince Charitable Trusts; Rosemary Kennedy Education Fund; Dr. Deborah Rose and Dr. Jan A. J. Stolwijk; Rosenthal Family Foundation; Mr. and Mrs. Albert H. Small; The Stella Boyle Smith Trust; Target; The Embassy of the United Arab Emirates; The Volgenau Foundation; Volkswagen Group of America; Dennis & Phyllis Washington; Wells Fargo; William R. Kenan, Jr. Charitable Trust; and generous contributors to the Abe Fortas Memorial Fund and by a major gift to the fund from the late Carolyn E. Agger, widow of Abe Fortas.

The content of this program may have been developed under a grant from the U.S. Department of Education but does not necessarily represent the policy of the U.S. Department of Education. You should not assume endorsement by the federal government.

Photography, Joanna McKee. Partial Copyediting, Jody Stokes-Casey. Some funding provided by the College of Fine + Applied Arts at the University of Illinois, Urbana-Champaign.

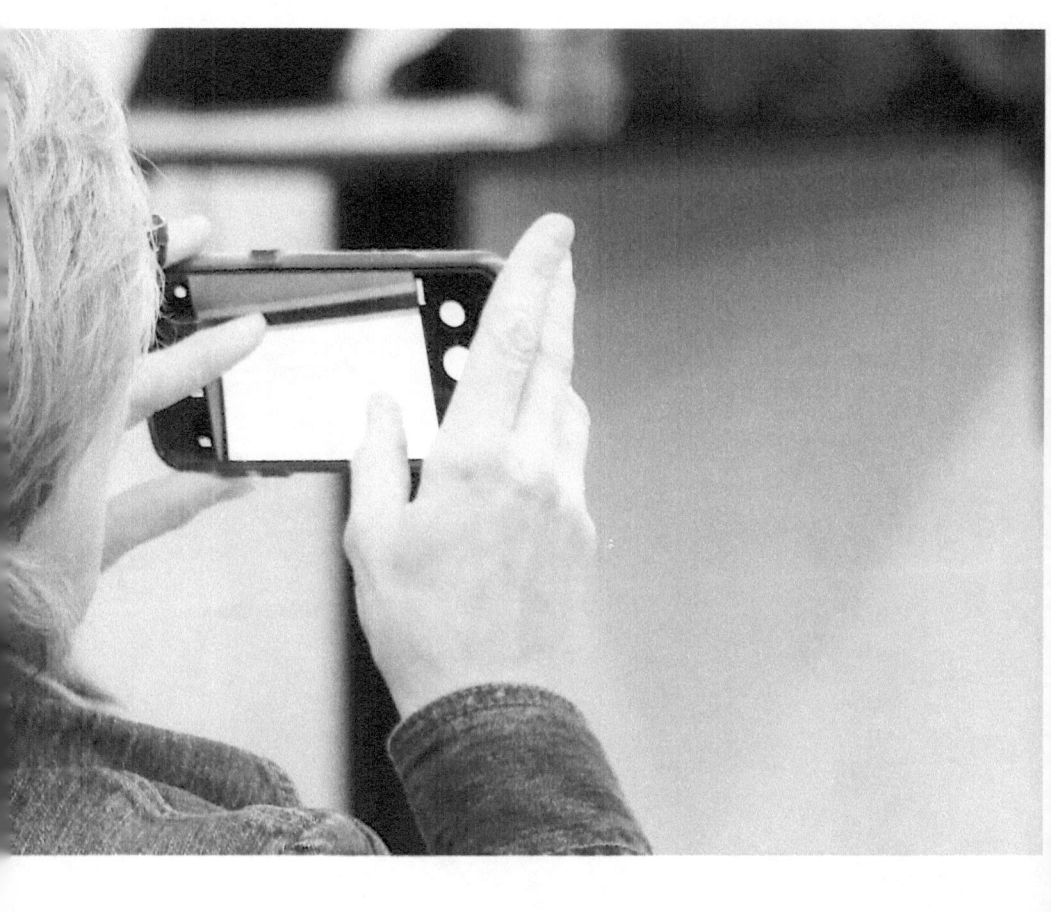

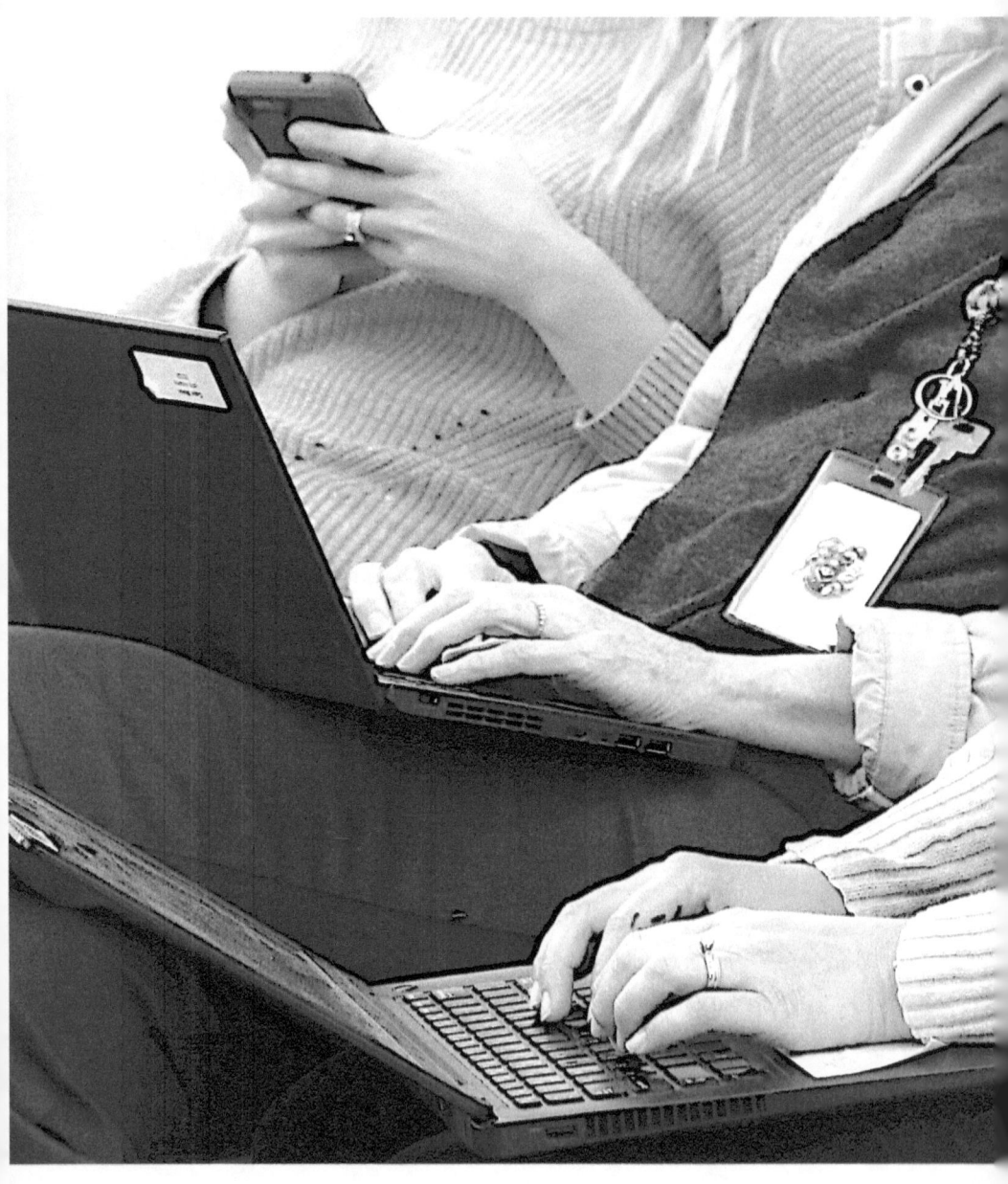

~ CONTENTS ~

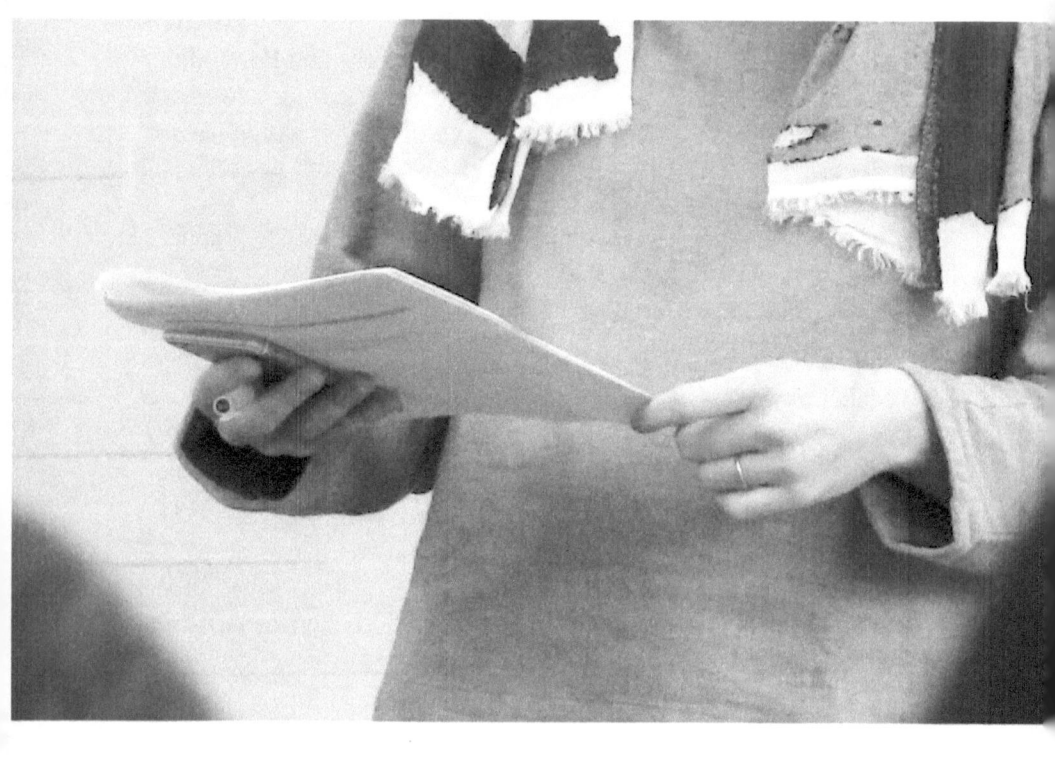

~ PREFACE ~

On September 7, 2019, the Kennedy Center experienced a historic change with the opening of the REACH. The intention of our expanded campus has been to provide a space for the public that allows audience and art to collide, revealing the artistic process in real time. What was once typically exclusive to the performer, can now be broken down and examined through open, light-filled spaces and exploratory programming in education.

For a center known for delivering beautifully finished products, there was a new challenge for our staff – how do we as curators and educators take a step back and let the audience jump in as collaborators? How do we live in the unfinished, unresolved messiness that is the artistic process and embrace that as the desired product?

With these questions driving our work, we approached our school and community's season of learning with a determination for change. Bringing in Jorge Lucero, conceptual artist and professor, as a presenter for a teacher professional workshop not only provided us a new voice but a shift in perspective. When I read Jorge's proposed title for the workshop, "Teacher as Artist-in-Residence: The Most Radical Form of Expression to Ever Exist" I laughed aloud. The audacity of the title made light of our request that Jorge shake things up for our programming of the classroom spaces in the REACH but I felt confident in our decision to stay with the title.

A radical expression of learning did happen that night. Jorge Lucero empowered you, the teachers, to jump in as equals and as collaborators. You, the teachers, were experts who shared the minutia of your life, your schools, your classrooms and your students, in order to find artistic expression within your own daily practices.

Ultimately, I want to thank you, the collaborators, for taking the first step in becoming part of the Kennedy Center's grand experiment that is the REACH. Thank you to Jorge for being a part of this journey and showing us that the unfinished, unresolved messiness of the artistic process can be a wonderful place to exist as an audience member, an artist and most importantly, as an educator.

Erica Palmiter
Manager, Teaching Artist Strategy
John F. Kennedy Center for the Performing Arts

~ INTRODUCTION ~

Seedlings

I delivered a version of the lecture "Teacher as Artist-in-Residence" at the John F. Kennedy Center for the Performing Arts on December 2, 2019. A revised version of that lecture is chapter one of this book. The lecture at the Kennedy Center was followed by a ninety-minute workshop, wherein thirty-three teachers from Washington DC, Maryland, and Virginia wrote chapters two through seven of this book. Yes, thirty-three teachers wrote the majority of this book in 90 minutes. The book primarily archives a momentary sampling of the participating teachers' expertise, framed by the six conceptual writing prompts that I presented to them during the workshop. These prompts—each explained in the blurbs located at the beginning of each corresponding chapter—engendered seedlings from the participating teachers' current and accumulated observations, fascinations, knowledge, wisdom, questions, dreams, and common sense.

As such, everything in this book—including the opening lecture—is presented, not as a closed and fully-formed statement or idea, rather as a mere seedling. A seedling differs from a seed because—although still in its infancy—it is already sprouting. Yes, these seedlings are small—maybe even easily ignored in their obviousness—but the seedlings are very much alive, their little green hands extending through the dirt towards the warmth of our inextinguishable imaginations. This book is an overgrown greenhouse and the reader of the book is invited to take the seedlings sprouting here and tend to them in their own creative, pedagogical, and civic gardens. The sprouts in this book are magic seedlings.

You will notice that the co-authored chapters (2-7) have no indication as to who wrote what. Everything that was contributed by the teachers to those parts of the book have been collated and rearranged to form—as it were—a single poetic sequence from one seedling of expertise to another. This was done deliberately to fool the memory. It is important for any user of this book (the authors themselves, but—of course—any other reader as well) to not-know where any given seedling of expertise came from, therefore—perhaps—allowing themselves to think that they contributed that seeding to this book. This muddied sense of where an idea may have come from, opens up the seedling to generativity. This is just another way of saying that something—anything—can happen when a given resource is open-ended enough to be played with.

About chapter one
Chapter one in this book started with the bones of the lecture I gave at the Kennedy Center on December 2, 2019. This new written version of the lecture is denser than it would come across in person. In person, I would show you images of artworks I've made that demonstrate how I've been working through some of

these ideas. I would attempt to make funny comments. There would be opportunity for conversation and I would be able to see your face. Seeing your face would let me know which threads to pull on and which ones to leave for another time. Delivering a lecture or artist talk in person allows the pedagogy of dialogue to be performed. Giving a lecture is truly an act of theatre, not because it's dramatic or because it is inherently artificial (both of which it is), rather because as the shared etymology of the words *theatre* and *theory* propose, both are occurrences that need **to be beheld**. It is easy for us to accept that theatre needs to be beheld because this is how we're used to engaging it. We mostly sit and watch it happen. Theatre—both live and cinematic—washes over us. We feel it. We are less convinced when it comes to theory because we associate theory with something that happens in school and we have come to an erroneous sensibility about school, that it is a place where you go to get stuff (e.g. knowledge, skills, accreditations, trivia, etc.). We attribute our intelligence—which is inherently dynamic—to what we have managed to *get* in state mandated blocks of time through a mostly prescribed and stagnant curriculum. Theory, however, is not to be gotten or owned the way you would a trophy, a medal, or a grade for that matter. School assumes sameness; theory expects difference. Theory is meant to be lived with, not unlike theatre. We're meant to come back to it repeatedly, each time having a somewhat different—maybe even personal—experience with it. This is how we learn from theory: *We behold it*. We

walk away somewhat confused, somewhat curious—
sometimes informed, but mostly in the process of
formation. We then live our lives and things happen to
us, personal things, entertaining things, supernatural
things. We encounter other kinds of theory, in a
plethora of shapes, sizes, and medias. And we have
these encounters with theory in relation to all sorts of
content. The whole experience is an interconnected
dynamic network with no indication as to where it
begins or where it ends. It has its moments of linearity,
but it is not linear. It has its moments of stillness but it
is not concrete.

As we move through time, we may—at another
moment—pull the theory off the shelf again or we
may hear a lecture or a poem based on that same idea
we came across way back when. At this point—based
on that life we've been living in the meantime—this
old, seemingly frozen, theory that we were confused
by before seems to either make more *or* different
sense. Maybe at this point what we're reading or
hearing catches us in a moment of serendipity or
divine revelation and we feel fuller, more articulated,
and ready to go. That theory—wherever we beheld
it—then becomes a part of our vocabulary and we use
it to not only make sense of the world, but to make
sense in the world. We put it on our list of most
influential ideas. Doesn't this sound like I'm
describing the kind of experience we have with songs
we play on a loop, meals we had a restaurant that we
like to go back to, or movies we re-watch, quote from,
and basically use as guiding texts in our lives? The

properties of the tune, meal or movie don't actually change. We change. This is how we live with theory. When you read my lecture/essay take it as a piece of theory or as a piece of art (same thing). You may get something from it when you read it for the first time. You may get little. Whatever happens, that's okay. Hopefully there is time to come back to it. What is most important is that you know that in the midst of the theory I'm presenting in chapter one, I'm saying that teachers are experts and that expertise—through the permissions of conceptual art—can propel us (teachers/artists) to be the premiere artist-in-residence in our own educative spaces (e.g. schools, homes, public squares, places of worship, online communities, etc.). I'm also positing that teaching is the most sophisticated form of conceptual art practice that has ever been made, particularly when it is invisible—which I propose is most of the time.

Thank you

I couldn't be more grateful to all the people that made this collaboration with the Kennedy Center possible. First and foremost, thank you to Erica Palmiter for bringing it to fruition and for trusting the process and the content along the way. Thanks to Nate Diamond for the original invitation and for thinking about me, even after all these years. Thanks to Lauren Flynn for making all the logistics of the trip and the project feel completely painless. I loved walking pass the Watergate every morning. Of course, thanks to Mario Rossero, my dear friend. I'm glad I got to catch you at the tail end of your stint at the Kennedy Center and

I'm now looking forward to what I anticipate will be your long and fruitful tenure with the National Art Education Association.

I had a great time in DC and I'm grateful to everyone who made it such a rejuvenating trip for me. Thanks to Amy Oswalt, Emily Courtney, and Colleen Cavanagh from the Washington DC Lab School for— not only inviting me to tour your amazing school—but also for taking me to the Glenstone and to the Old Angler Inn. It was a perfect way to start the trip. Since this project came at the end of an eight-month sabbatical from my responsibilities at the University of Illinois I am so grateful for the support I received from my colleagues and students in the School of Art + Design and in the College of Fine and Applied Arts. This project is—in part—possible because of that support. Thank you to Alan Mette, my Director and Kevin Hamilton, my Dean.

Even though this book project was initiated and completed in December of 2019, it has been in-progress for a few years now. Four invitations during my sabbatical (and one before it) have been particularly vital in helping me—not only formulate the ideas in the lecture—but also understand what the DC teachers and I are trying to collectively present in the chapters (2-7) that emerged from the workshop at the Kennedy Center. The importance of finding kin in the work one is doing cannot be overstated. I can't imagine this book existing without the conviviality and collaboration around *Teacher as Conceptual*

Artist, that I've shared with Emiel Heijnen, Melissa Bremmer and Sanne Kersten from the Amsterdam University of the Arts. Thanks to John Bakker and Ryan Thompson at Trinity Christian College for inviting me to make a "book in a day" with your students; Joe Ostraff and Dan Barney at BYU for letting me come and give a version of this lecture in Provo; Christopher Schulte, Angela LaPorte, Injeong Yoon, and Alphonso Grant for your generous invitation to workshop some of these ideas at the University of Arkansas; and Laura Shaeffer at Compound Yellow for inviting me to put on the YOURSTUFF Museum exhibition, which is a concurrent experiment in highlighting *everydayness* as expertise. There are pieces of all our conversations throughout this project.

The photographs in this book are by Joanna McKee, photographer at the Kennedy Center. Thanks for letting me use (and crop) your pictures. Thank you to Jody Stokes-Casey from the University of Illinois who helped with copyediting of all the teacher portions in this book. The way you organized the sections is so careful. You made the seedlings into poems.

Of course, I am forever indebted to my family for their unwavering—above and beyond—support: Maribel, Jorge, Lucas, Mateo, and Lucia. I love you.

Finally, this book only exists because of the rich contributions of the teachers who participated in the project. From here on out, say to people, "I wrote a book".

Thank you Kevin Allen, Maria Barreda, Jaime Carroll, Michelle Choman, Emily Courtney, Miriam Cutelis, Mackenzie Escobar, Lynn Gudhus, Melinda Hale, Jennifer Hesla, Tami E. Johnson, Jordan Kivitz, Ana Celina Knez, Joanna Lewton, Gaye Makin, Janet Mays, Mary Ruth McGinn, Jennifer Messman, Amy Oswalt, Andrea Perll, Tahmena Rauf, Adzua Robinson, Suzy Scollon, C.Renee Seay, Banafsheh Shearer, Emily Shepardson, Johab Silva, Elizabeth Snead, Hannah Topka, Lauren Tredinnick, Rebecca Winner, and Anna Zwegat.

Jorge Lucero
January, 2020

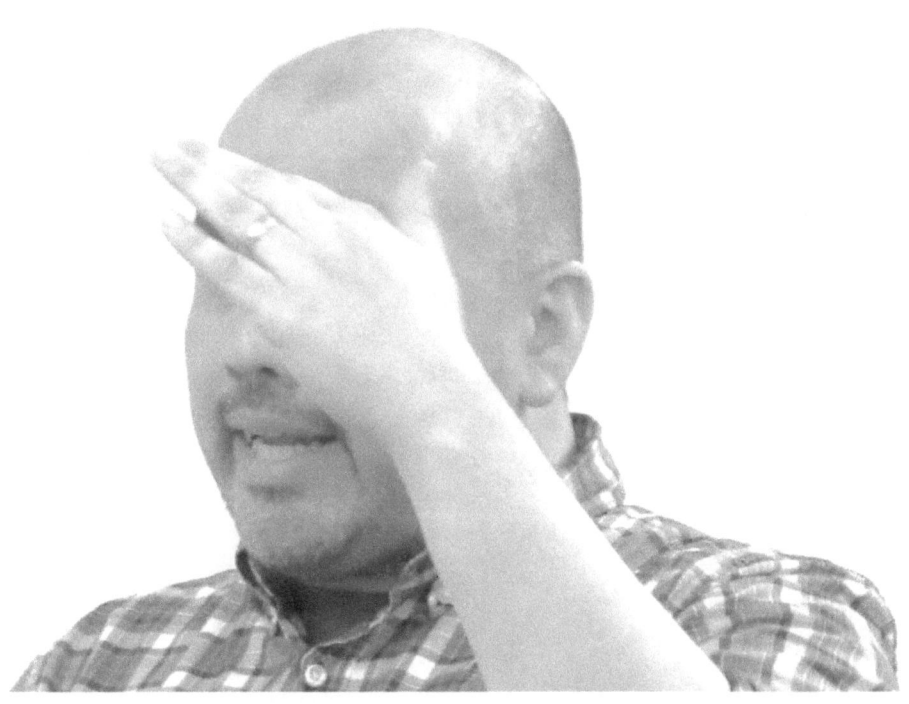

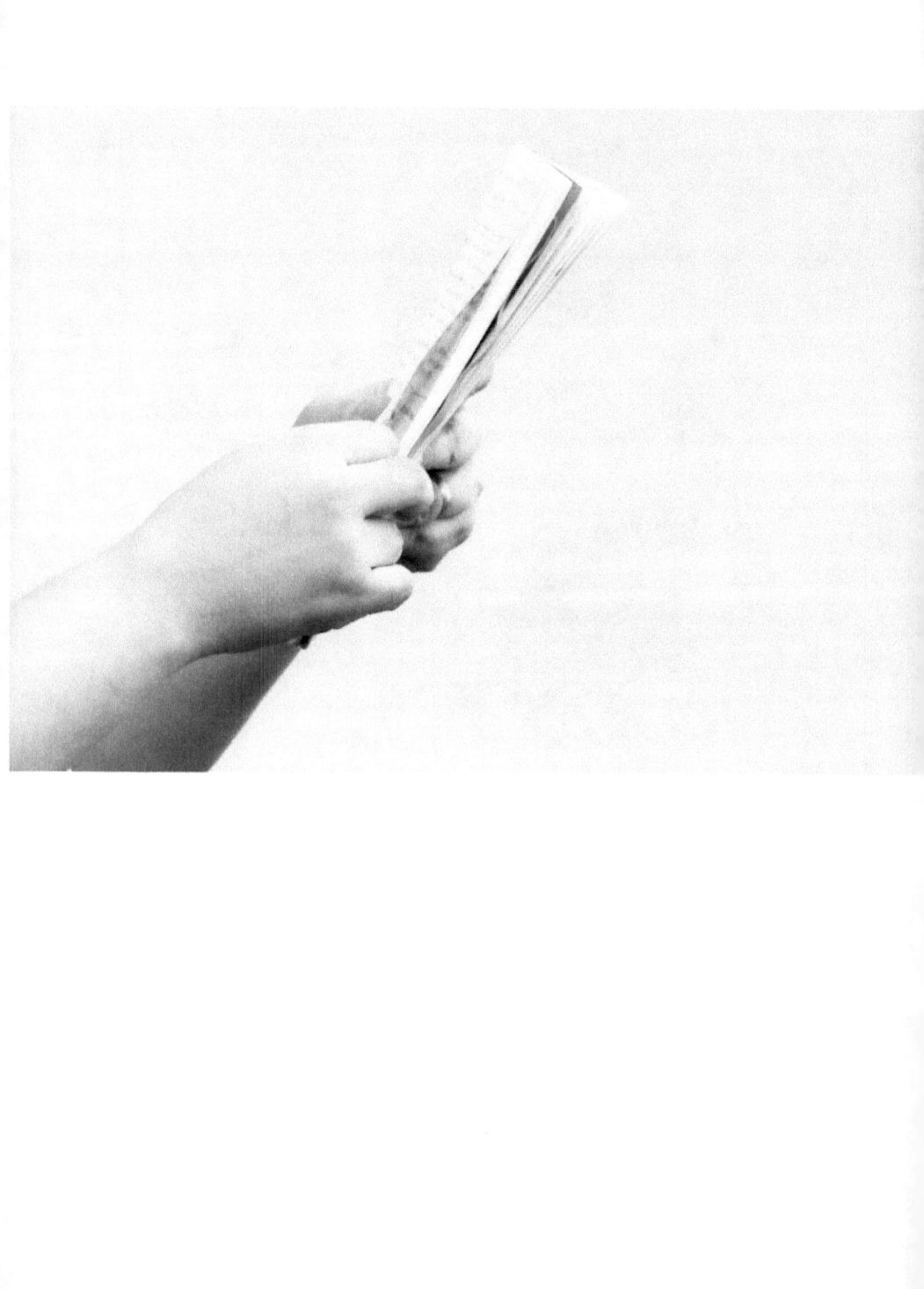

[1]

TEACHER AS ARTIST-IN-RESIDENCE
*Thoughts on expertise and
conceptual art permissions for daily living*

Jorge Lucero

When I was invited to give this lecture at the Kennedy Center I was asked to write a description that could be used to promote both it and its accompanying workshop. I sent our hosts the following description expecting that it would get kicked-back to me with understandable suggestions to either qualify or tone down my hyperbole.

Teacher as Artist-in-Residence: The most radical form of expression to ever exist.

What if there was a way of thinking about our own teaching as an art practice and what if that teaching-as-art-practice was the most radical form of expression to ever exist? For many teachers, arts-integration frequently involves collaboration with an external expert, but what if teachers themselves became the artist-in-residence in their own classrooms? How do teachers who don't readily identify as creative practitioners use the expertise they already have and the activities they already *do* as a means to activate a robust and sustainable arts integration practice that permeates both the curriculum AND the teacher's entire posture as an educator, citizen, and person? By dismantling long-held ideas about expertise, productivity, and art itself, this lecture and workshop proposes a pathway for teachers to permanently exist as creative practitioners in their own classrooms and

22

> schools. Other than *thinking*, there is no special art skill requirement for teachers to emerge as the premiere artists-in-residence in their classrooms.

The proposal for my lecture and workshop never came back to me for revisions. The next time I saw it was a few months ago, when it was printed in the promotional materials for my visit to the Kennedy Center. So, it looks like I have set up a tall order for myself and now I have to deliver. What could I possibly show you that is the "most radical form of expression to ever exist"?

Well, right away, I should say that what I'm going to talk about isn't anything new, although I will try to make an argument for how it is—in fact—radical (meaning, "having to do with roots"). *Teacher as Artist-in-Residence* is first a posture of paying close attention to latent or ignored expertise. This expertise is always there, in many different ways, at various sites where creative practice (or art) and education overlap. Second, *Teacher as Artist-in-Residence* is a reconceptualization of how the teacher sees themselves within the whole educational enterprise (including schooling, parenting, civic engagement, etc.). It's a move beyond being a professional educator, towards understanding oneself as a creative practitioner within the parameters of one's teaching occupation and/or practice, by seeing oneself as an artist everywhere and always.

To do this I'll be talking a lot about conceptual art. Through the permissions of conceptual art, I will unearth what is "radical" in teaching; I will rethink the ordinary as a means to open up *who* gets to be an artist-in-residence; I'll examine *where*, *how*, and *when* art occurs; and ultimately, what new forms of expression emerge when conceptual art and education intersect.

Who is an expert?

The expertise I'll be talking about today is something that every person hearing these words already carries with them. It is something that we don't usually think of as expertise because it appears too ordinary to be thought of as specialized or honed knowledge. It is also a kind of expertise that is not necessarily attached to a profession. When someone is an expert they seemingly know a lot about a certain subject or they are confident enough in their prior experiences with a subject or gesture to engage it repeatedly, anticipating fairly predictable results. Dedicated individuals with degrees, titles, occupations, and achievements in specific areas of natural and created phenomena are the kinds of experts we're used to seeing. These are people we look to in order to fill the gaps in our knowledge. We also look to them to validate—with their presumably vetted credentials—the knowledge we're constructing.

A more generous definition, which is less anchored to publicly recognized notions of expertise, could be that an expert is simply someone who uniquely knows something about something. People who carry this type of expertise may not readily call themselves experts and may even point to their blind-spots in a given topic in order to shed off the responsibility of having to represent it. This humble posture does not disqualify them though. I actually work in a place with a lot of people who are certified experts and the best of them are the ones who are fully aware that they have gaps in their knowledge. After all, the true expert is a dynamic creature perpetually evolving over time, patiently inching through vast—maybe infinite—worlds. They are motivated less by the attainment or perpetuation of their credentials and more by a hungry curiosity triggered by a deep belief (or anxiety?) that there is always something else.

In trying to demonstrate—or perhaps uncover—where expertise is hidden, I sometimes ask groups that I'm working with to close their eyes, pretend that they're holding a pencil, and then write their signature on an imaginary piece of paper in the air. Everyone—without fail—does it. I then ask them to do it five times, repeatedly. Each person does it masterfully and without hesitation. The embodied and effortless signature of each individual is always a unique, sophisticated *drawing* made—not just once—but multiple times with magnificent exactitude, by a person with their eyes closed. This exercise magnifies expertise that is so quotidian (or everyday) that it mostly goes unnoticed. Because we understand this—almost banal—gesture of writing/drawing one's own signature as "second nature", we often miss the opportunity to see ourselves as people who have learned complex skills over time, perform sophisticated (dare I say, artistic) gestures on a daily basis, and carry within each and every one of us, a wonderous one-of-a-kind expertise.

The idea that everyday gestures and knowledge can be understood as creative expertise is a flattening of — not only hierarchies of knowledge — but also of art hierarchies. Most of our long-held ideas about what counts as art are actually lockstep with our understandings of what counts as expertise. Both art and expertise are rooted in distinctions of learned skills, workmanship, labor, and professional preparation (mostly through some form of education). In the world of art, conceptual art destabilizes these paradigms the most. In *Teacher as Artist-in-Residence* I aim to tease out — through the permissions of conceptual art — that the teacher is uniquely positioned as an expert and artist in their own classroom. Yes, of their content area — and hopefully of certain pedagogies — but also as an expert of their particular *everydayness*.

The teacher brings a ton of know-how, memory, skills, curiosities, strategies for scholarship/science, personality traits, tastes, beliefs, and experiences into their classroom. They've read things, watched movies and TV, taken trips, cooked hundreds of meals, fixed things, invented games, made arrangements, felt emotions, had thoughts, taken shortcuts, doubted, worshiped, solved problems, written, and expressed themselves in countless ways of which only a few may have involved words. All this in addition to whatever formal schooling the teacher went through. This person, the fully enriched, alive teacher is in relation to their equally alive students on a day to day basis and through this durational gesture of being together, they reciprocate one to another. The teacher's expertise and queries—both related and unrelated to being at school—course through and around them. They then carry them down the hallway into every interaction they have with students, colleagues, staff members, parents, and other community stakeholders. The whole thing is constant and indeterminate and teachers are masters at it. The students are really good at it too, bringing their worlds (their expertise) into those spaces. In this way, the students and the teacher are each other's contemporaries in a highly sophisticated, felt, and lively interplay that has been enacted throughout the ages, but infrequently leveraged as an art practice in and of itself.

In the next part I'm going to talk about how conceptual art disrupted the hierarchies of art and expertise, and how this now opens up permissions for *Teacher as Artist-in-Residence*. But before I do that I just want to add a caveat about what it might mean to recognize oneself as an expert/artist within a school. This posture is not territorial. It is not meant to keep others and their difference out of our spaces. *Teacher as Artist-in-Residence* is a realization that should enhance how a teacher sees themselves in relation to every other creative practitioner, professional, and layperson with expertise-to-share that might potentially want to partner with a teacher and their students. Yes, we (teachers and students) are the primary authors and inhabitants of the culture that others may want to be a part of—our school culture—but a recognition of that position shouldn't make us afraid, unwelcoming, or arrogant. The old "visiting artist" paradigm follows the "master class" model: An outside expert comes to our space for a few hours or days and teaches their ideas— through their pedagogy—to our community, usually independent of whatever preceded or follows their visit. *Teacher as Artist-in-Residence* proposes that if a visiting artist or scholar were to be invited into our space, it is not so that the teacher can take a back seat and merely observe this expert helicoptering their concerns, strategies, and ideas into our space. What might be more favorable is a visitor who might contribute to the ongoing work(s) that we already enact in that room on a daily basis. It is a meeting of experts: The teacher expert, the student expert, and— sometimes—invited outside experts.

Conceptual art's permissions for *Teacher as Artist-in-Residence*

Conceptual art presents a challenge to many ideas we may have about beauty, labor/craft, worth/value, archivalness, creative genius, politics, and even time, space, and reality. Conceptualist—as they are sometimes called—blur the line between art and everyday life readily, often causing confusion about what is what. They test the pliability not only of physical materials, but of time/duration, science/ learning, action/inaction, policy, relationships, chance/fate, entropy/formlessness, space, language, and documentation.

What follows as the major strategies for *Teacher as
Artist-in-Residence* are intimately related to another
ongoing work I've been engaged with for about
twenty years, *Teacher as Conceptual Artist* (see
Further Readings at the end of the book). Through
Teacher as Conceptual Artist I propose that teachers
and artists examine their shared modes-of-operation to
garner permissions for a hybrid practice that is
simultaneously progressive pedagogy *and* conceptual
art. Those shared modes include — but are not limited
to — negotiating relationality, testing the materiality of
time, recognizing the body politic *and* the politics of
bodies, theorizing the complexity and incompleteness
of documentation, foregrounding the tense discourse
between word and object, and pursuing a constant —
almost utopian — aspiration for being wide-eyed in the
world for the sake *of* the world. By identifying where
conceptual artists' and teachers' modes-of-operation
share intentions, vocabulary, and strategies, both
teachers *and* artists can come to see their otherwise
separate practices as the same activity.

So — for example — a teacher as conceptual artist in a
school may begin to see the materiality of things,
relationships, and activities within the school that
aren't typically understood as artist's material. These
materials then get tested for expressive and experimental
pliability and potential. What is the materiality of a passing
period? Of an attendance record, of a parent-teacher
conference, of a photocopier, of a teacher in-service, of
security and disciplinary procedures, of the school building
and grounds themselves? This can be an interminable

list opened up through the permissions of conceptual art (see Chapter 2 of this book).

For centuries—and still in the general public's collective expectation—art has to be *a thing*, an actual object or event to look at. Conceptual art pushes against that rule. Put plainly, conceptual art foregrounds the idea over the object or event in an art work. Sometimes that means whatever the artist is doing is all in service of communicating their idea(s). As such, in some conceptual art, typical artistic gestures (e.g. designing, making, presenting) get minimized, de-aestheticized, or eliminated in order to emphasize the act of communication. Whatever is being called art by the conceptual artist, could actually be lacking a physical, handmade, or archival presence and could—in the end—just be the artist's existence by itself. In this case, the driving idea offers the parameters for an artistic stance by the artist, without having to "make" anything in a conventional sense. The conceptual artist then is a cross-disciplinary polyglot ("speaker" of many languages) whose every move could potentially be their art work.

Arguably, all art—across time and geography— contains ideas, but it is only since the mid-1910s that art can be argued to be conceptual. Even artists who made representational artworks or argued for pure formalism in their work during the 20th Century couldn't help but take their position in relation to the intimations of their conceptual art counterparts. The apex of "big C" Conceptual Art was—arguably—the

1960s and in this flurry of activity, the theorist Lucy
Lippard threw down a gauntlet, which has yet to be
taken up completely by any one artist or group of
artists. In their essay *The Dematerialization of the Art
Object*, Lippard and co-author John Chandler,
demarcated a final frontier for conceptual (and maybe
all) forms of expression. They reflected:

> We still don't know how much less
> nothing can be.

For the last sixty years, both directly and indirectly,
this has been the artworld's challenge: To try to
occupy the realm between art and life, between object
and idea, and between the visible and the invisible.
Logically, if we ever finally "know how much less
nothing can be", we may not even know it. After all,
isn't *less nothing* undocumentable and therefore
imperceptible?

Documentation is both the limit and the lifeblood of
conceptual art. As hinted to just now, documentation is
what keeps us from going over the edge of experimentation
in conceptual art. Even if that documentation is something
as immaterial and fleeting as the verbal recounting of one
person who witnessed the work, this is enough to keep it
from reaching that realm of *less nothing*. Equally,
photography, video, writing, audio recordings, and
ancillary artifacts all aid in the archiving of, academic
study, creative response, and cultural discourse around
conceptual art. Documentation keeps conceptual art
present and accessible to those of us who want to learn

from it, even though it is that very documentation that triggers the catch-22 of the pursuit of *less nothing*.

Artists who have gotten close to the line of *less nothing*, but have fallen short because of the slipperiness of documentation have made a lot of work that opens up permissions for teachers who want to take a *Teacher as Artist-in-Residence* posture within their schools. Thank God for their "failed" attempts.

The pursuit of *less nothing* as the most radical form of expression to ever exist

The *everydayness* of teaching offers something useful to the provocation of "knowing how much less nothing can be". *Everydayness* can be thought of as an adjective and a noun. As an adjective it can be used to describe what is plainly before us on a daily basis, though many times these occurrences, things, sentiments, and gestures are invisible. As a noun, we can think of everydayness as a material that can be made pliable for the sake of shear curiosity or—dare we say—expression (e.g. art). In teaching, the oscillation between the invisibility of *everydayness* and its pliability is a site of radicality that we can now wade into for the sake of conducting a teaching practice that is simultaneously a creative practice. When I was talking about latent expertise a moment ago, I was pointing to this: The materiality of the everyday.

Everydayness is both ordinary and vital. Uncovered ordinariness is truly radical because it reveals the interconnected, underground tubers that control everything. Ordinariness put on display still seems to scandalize the general public. That's unfortunate because sometimes the sensationalism of the uncovering makes us more jaded with art than we are with other forms of discovery. A little over a hundred years ago Marcel Duchamp notoriously did it with his *readymades*. The presentation of a mass-market, factory-made, catalog-bought urinal as if it were a porcelain sculpture still elicits a collective groan from most of my undergraduate classes. Just this year, 2019, another artist Maurizio Cattelan made it into many of the late-night comedy monologues by presenting a similar idea, a real banana adhered to a wall with a piece of duct tape. Understandably, the ordinariness and—maybe—ease of the gesture still causes a shock in a public that wants their artists to specialize in feats of refined skill. But these ordinary gestures presented as art—are less on par with acrobatics—and more like a biologist inviting you over to peer through their microscope. The moves by Duchamp, Cattelan and thousands of others is to take something that is a thing in the world—perhaps an ignored or taken for granted thing—and through the permission of art put a bracket or parenthesis around it. In other words, to discover *it*. This is about the only experimental move you can still pull in the art world. Be ordinary. Be *less nothing*.

The conceptual art gesture many times is simply to say, "I'm showing you *this*"—as one of John Baldessari's early conceptualist works nakedly declares, *All Conceptual Art is Just Pointing at Things*. So, when I first started working through this lecture—I was asking, "what obvious thing can I point out that is both ordinary and vital?" I wanted to point out that teachers are experts and that this expertise can be understood as an art practice, and also that *this* art practice—if recognized and committed to—makes them/us the most important, influential person in our school building(s) or communities. Radical means root, the core which is hidden and underneath. We can then understand radical—not as something that is more true, newer, or more impactful—rather as something that matures and becomes spectacular underground, out-of-sight, and over a mostly ignored duration. The expertise of *Teacher as Artist-in-Residence* is radical because it is ordinary, but when revealed, pulled out, harvested, and pointed out; it shows its colors, its size, its uniqueness, its interconnectedness, and its essential vitality.

The other part of all this has to do with the fact that the thing I was claiming—the importance of teacher as expert in their own teaching and learning spaces—was not a claim I was making solely within the context of the school, but rather since school is life, the role of the *Teacher as Artist-in-Residence* is the most important artistic gesture that is made in the lived world.

The durational, invisible work of teaching
For some, *Teacher as Artist-in-Residence* or *Teacher as Conceptual Artist* can be incredibly troubling

because these proposals simultaneously position teaching and conceptual art as both ordinary and vital. This pairing at first appears as a contradiction, but being a teacher not only takes patience and an unshakable trust in the process; it undoubtedly requires its participants to be both fully present in the moment, while always being cognizant of the cosmic immeasurability of the wider enterprise we call education. The imperceptibility of teaching—not unlike the imperceptibility of conceptual art—is caused by its ordinariness and size (both physical and temporal). You see, teaching is a durational (life-long) project that individual teachers take up with the full knowledge that each of them is nothing more than a single contributor to something they'll never see in its entirety. We teachers are but one node in a wild rhizome (a web of roots), one paragraph in a student's lifelong narrative. Counterintuitively, we're at peace about our inability to see the beginning, the middle, and the end. We're content having been one part of a larger trajectory. Teaching is mostly an invisible practice. The conceptual artist shares this disposition towards the perennial and the *not-seen*.

For our purposes it is merely important to recognize that teachers do a lot of methodical, unflashy work that poignantly reverberates culturally, economically, politically, relationally, and spiritually. Through the permissions of conceptual art, the work of the teacher, alongside their students, can be understood as a truly sophisticated, robust, and unique work of durational and dematerialized art (which is the term Lippard popularized to describe art works taking up the *less nothing* challenge).

The majority of what teachers do alongside their students is—undoubtedly—invisible practice. Through conceptual art we can start to think of these invisible practices as creative practice and therefore the most radical form of expression that has ever existed. Take for example the customary 40-week American school year. During this time a teacher prepares, delivers, assesses, and modifies a curriculum over and over from day 1 to day 280. That is the job of a teacher at least on paper. Simultaneously, this same teacher carries out the multiple roles of counselor, parent/guardian, nurse, coach, custodian, handy-person, therapist/psychologist, colleague, administrator, police, co-learner, mad-scientist, storyteller, zoologist, philosopher, referee, advocate, tour-guide, scholar, chef, and friend. Perhaps, there is some documentation of the school year, a digital folder on a school-administered laptop with some jpegs in it. If the teacher is excellent at it, the documentation is a collection of highlights from the year: fieldtrips, hot lunches, special guests, holidays, pep rallies, school dances, and student work. Maybe the teacher has shot some candid photos of students working together or simply living life alongside each other. By obligation, most teachers may have saved documents with written self-reflections, their teaching-philosophies, lesson-plans, worksheets, rubrics, documentation about undesirable student behavior, forms that have been filled out (for special events, requests, or incidents), and attendance records. That's it. The tip of the gargantuan, immeasurable iceberg. A small representation of a life lived together enacting the collective enterprise of—at worst—enculturation and—at best—communally making what Hannah Arendt envisioned as "an adequate home in the world".

Teaching occurs non-spectacularly hence our use of terms like core, foundational, exam and test, which all allude to an unearthing type of activity. Curriculum in and of itself is something that runs under the surface. It courses through the veins of our teaching posture and practice. What happens under the surface is the main materiality of teaching, learning, and schooling. Teachers and students enact a heavily relational, long, and naturally abstract activity that is both cosmically transformative and inevitable. Learning seems to be propelled by life itself. Sure, the form of teaching and learning (aka pedagogy) remains in flux, changing— maybe imperceptibly—from moment to moment, but teaching and learning is what we are made of and paying attention to it as a type of pliable material has the potential of—indeed—achieving the challenge that Lippard and Chandler left us. It is in this realm of the invisibility of school that a pathway opens up for teachers to identify as conceptual artist and for artist to recognize how close to knowing "how much less nothing can be" teaching is.

To be alive
Good teaching and good conceptual art are like gardening. They are not only invisible, they are alive, ever-present, and mostly independent from whoever has convinced themselves that they are the ones who control the situation. It is true, both teaching and

conceptual art sometimes enlist the services of a tiller—meaning, one who agitates and prepares the soil—and sometimes they require the services of a tender—or one who guards the process—but on the whole, wildness takes over. We (teachers/artists) do a few things and then we wait and watch. Borrowing an adage from the British artist Martin Creed, (which he says he stole from Gerhard Richter) *Teacher as Artist-in-Residence* is—in the end— "stupid like nature". It's not meant pejoratively though. What Creed is acknowledging is the indeterminacy of nature and how he aspires for that in his work. Creed is pointing to aliveness.

Modes-of-operation: For tilling and tending

So what gestures does conceptual art open up for the teacher to till the soil and tend the garden of their practice as an *Artist-in-Residence*? In every art form—from filmmaking to cooking; from writing to teaching—I have witnessed the encouragement of playing with materials (e.g. sources, parts, strategies, traditions, stuff) as a means to find the edges of expression. Directors encourage improvisation. Musicians create mash-ups. Writers jot down from their stream of consciousness. A teacher makes an exception, interrupting that day's plans in deference to emergent events, issues, questions, and teachable moments. We prompt others in their creative work by coaching them to "play" because playing—at first—appears to be a low-stakes game. Sharing an etymological root, *play* and *ply* mean the same thing: to fold or bend. Pliability is an act of testing out a material's point of resistance. Where will a given material not let you push it anymore? When will it push back? What will this confrontation produce? The question I ask in the posture of *Teacher as Artist-in-Residence* and *Teacher as Conceptual Artist* is what can be material and how can we test its pliability?

To end this lecture, I would like to parse out eleven modes-of-operation that I've identified as permissions from conceptual art practices. These modes of operation are meant for artists, which—I'll remind you—is meant to include teachers. As I mentioned earlier, there is no formula for the *Teacher as Artist-in-Residence* and I would hope that—true to the form of conceptualist practices across time and geography—that any definition made now would soon enough evolve into something else or be completely replaced in both thought and action. If you read the following eleven modes-of-operation as a didactic "how-to" you may be reading it in a way that will ultimately feel oppressive and not useful to your everyday living. However, if you read this next section as parameters that could be reacted to, then you may indeed find your own practice in the midst of all this theory. I would encourage you to play, to experiment, and to test the pliability of even these proposals. As conceptualist Allan Kaprow noted in his germinal 1997 thoughts on experimentation in art, *Just Doing*:

> Today, we may say that experimental art is that act or thought whose identity as art must always remain in doubt. Not only does

39

this hold for anyone who plays with the "artist"; it holds especially for the "artist"! The experiment is not to possess a secret artistry in deep disguise; it is not knowing what to call it at any time! As soon—and it is usually very soon—as such acts and thoughts are associated with art and its discoveries, it is time to move on to other possibilities of experimentation.

So, take what you like from what I'm proposing, see if it matches with your sensibility, study the works of others and reconceptualize the whole enterprise. It can't be avoided that these modes are listed in a sequence here, but they don't go one after the other. They're sometimes enacted all at the same time. Finally, in the pursuit of Lippard and Chandler's *less nothing* challenge and my proposal about what expertise can be for the *Teacher as Artist-in-Residence*, I would suggest that you look at what you already do and go from there. There's no need to add new tasks to your life. All that you need to do to be a *Teacher as Artist-in-Residence* is to understand yourself as a conceptual artist and this comes by merely putting brackets around what you already do. Call the things you do, "art".

Like things and think about why you like them
On the whole, "liking" something is seen as a pretty base form of expression. Without taking away its simplicity I also propose that we remember how unique and potent it is to have personal taste. After

this, we may begin to think about our ability to have discernment; to not only say "I like *this* or *that*", but to be able to construct ideas and relationships around the things we like. If you like something, ask yourself why you like it. Really think about this. Make top-ten lists if that helps. What does a top-ten list of your favorite comedy movies say that is different from your list of favorite grocery stores? A top-ten list is an arbitrary exercise, but it sets the boundaries by which you can think through your tastes. When I make these lists, I end up with eleven or twelve movies or grocery stores, which then means I have to have a conversation within myself (and sometimes with others) about why some movie or store was left off my list.

This isn't trivial. It brings to the fore our ability to decipher between qualities and really helps us to articulate ourselves as learners, as consumers of culture, and—even—as producers of thought and art. In thinking about what you like in such an analytical manner, you may begin to see patterns that tell you what kinds of things you like to think about and therefore what is important to you in the greater scheme of things. This kind of self-reflection might lead you to think about who your kin could be, and finding kin may be one of the single most important aspects of your practice as a teacher/artist. There is plenty of sage wisdom to buttress the idea of finding kinship—from bumper stickers to ancient religious texts—but we only have to look back at pairings or groups of artists, athletes, and inventors to see what

41

the significance of understanding your "likes" in relation to others could be. This proclivity of artists coming together around mutual likes is perhaps not that surprising, but a lot of teacher-practice is done in isolation even in the midst of fully populated school building and districts. Teaching is a creative practice, and *Teacher-as Artist-in-Residence* even more so. Know your likes, find your kin, and make your work.

Always be doing the "literature" review

Doing the literature review is a task that rules the academy. The results of doing a literature review can be found in almost every dissertation, thesis, published research paper, scholarly book, and academic presentation. The conventional expert—which I defined in an early part of this lecture—can be partially evaluated by the thoroughness of their literature review. But doing the literature review as a daily creative practice is not exclusive to academics. It is a means by which any dedicated person who wants to test the pliability of their practice grows the conceptual and formal vocabularies of whatever it is they do. It is simply asking the questions, "what are the things that inform my next step and how do I assemble them on purpose for the benefit of what I'm doing?" So, for example, if one is a teacher (like many of us), perhaps that person reads books and articles about teaching, but they also perk up when they hear references, metaphors, and ideas about teaching in other texts and medias. Similar to my

mode of paying attention to the things I like,
doing the literature review involves paying close
attention to everything that inform what I'm
doing. To be thorough in our literature review it
will be important to notice—not just the texts
designated to our fields—but all of the ancillary
texts, medias, utterances, and experiences that
orbit whatever it is we do.

It may go without saying, but when I say "text"
I don't only mean conventional printed words; I
mean any *thing* that is legible—from a baby's
cry to a pile of dirt. Understanding texts this
generously, we'll also have to examine texts
that—at the moment—appear completely
irrelevant to our pursuits. A teacher may indeed
read books and articles about curriculum,
pedagogy, classroom management, or
educational philosophy and policy, but since—
as suggested earlier—the teacher/artist is a
polyglot (a speaker of many "languages") then it
may be important for the literature review to be
compiled of everything, not just the field-
specific texts.

For what it's worth most of us assemble our
literature reviews without even knowing it. We
could look at our bookshelves, file cabinets, and
the search histories on our devices to reveal a
portion of the textual foundation we are always
building on, but we may also look at our
playlists, our collections of objects, our family

albums, our religious texts, our comedy bits, our junk drawers, our contact lists, our backyards, and maybe even our bank accounts to examine what our practice is made of and where it's going.

There is a further step though, and that is the discipline of actively collecting and organizing your literature/textual review. When we discover what texts make up the literature review of our practice we then need to pursue that content on purpose. We need to become the librarians and curators of our own niche-practice. If there's something we find curious about a certain thing or phenomenon, we may then have to pair it with other similar findings. The collections, much like the traditional literature reviews, offer us the opportunity to go back and look at what we've assembled. We can then ask "why are these two things near each other?" and this will then open up unforeseen paths by which our practice as a *Teacher as Artist-in-Residence* can go.

Find the pliability of the material-at-hand

This mode-of-operation is actually quite conventional. I've already spoken about what pliability is, the testing of how much something—anything—can bend. Artists throughout history and geography have actively tested the pliability of material. If I give a group of kids each a ball of clay without any guiding instruction, they instinctively test the pliability of that material. Whether they actively squeeze it or just let the clay transfer its cold moisture to their hand, the simple act of touching is teaching the toucher something. In the human-made-world, learning about something's pliability opens up the possibilities of that material. This is so easy to imagine when it comes to ancient materials such as clay that it may seem elementary to even talk about it. Well, in *Teacher as Artist-in-Residence*, which is thought of through a conceptual art permission, it is this testing of pliability that opens up the school as the material at hand. Through conceptual art we are able to examine how some things that seem non-pliable (e.g. the institution of American schooling or bureaucracies in general) bend, move, and are consequently reimagined and remade? In case you're wondering, almost everything is pliable. This testing of pliability is not always done through physical touch; rather it is a "push" or pressure applied through ideas made manifest. There may be a lot of things in the universe that cannot be physically altered, but everything can be conceptually altered. A mere idea can change reality. With this, we then can ask, "how does a teacher and their students make school into material so it can be radical expressions of the artists-in-residence?"

Here's a list I came up with in 2016. It's called *Make School Material*. It was previously published as a poster to benefit the Chicago Free School and then again as part of my 2018 artist residency at the Amsterdam University of the Arts.

Work with everything. Be with everyone. Test pliability. Share resources. Show all work, all the time. Ambitiously fail. Flux curricularly. Get near. Highlight every individual. Make pairs. Touch freely. Look twice. Bracket banality. Co-construct. Listen at length. Typeface your emails. Lecture generously. Rupture normal. Erase masterpieces. Forgive fearlessly. Avoid teacherly. Plant things. Build buffets. Love like amateurs. Push off of the standard. Research every-thing. Play aimlessly. Read comics seriously. Write nonsense. Mush words. Take yourself seriously. Make yourself a joke. Draw on fogged glass. Run around. Invent music. Individualize uniforms. Trip through the field. Carry selflessly. Cry every time. Watch slowly. Hold conviviality. Walk as science. Weave as seeking. Politicize your personal. Stack and pile. Study breathing. Breathe while studying. Contemplate presence. Cross borders wide-eyed. Collect vocabulary. Offer time. Study etymology. Make lists. Assess with mercy. Absurd your image. Look up and down. Sit purposefully. Invent constantly. Split your lunch. Enjoy incomprehensibility. Be quiet more. Owe only love. Kindred your kindness. MAKE SCHOOL MATERIAL

Read and write to think, not just to explain

As an artist and teacher who lives and works at the intersection of conceptual art and teaching, I write. Writing is an activity I treat like drawing. Writing is a means by which the bits of thoughts and feelings I have are made concrete enough to be edited. By this I simply mean that when I see my thoughts down on paper—whether it's through a drawing or a sentence—I am able to have more and different thoughts about what I was thinking. It's an iterative process of provocation, expansion, and editorship.

Reading and writing are not just a means by which we acquire knowledge and report on it. They are creative activities. Reading is a means of beholding. (As I describe in my take on theory in the introduction to this book), reading is not strictly for comprehension—as certain tests would have us believe—rather it is a means of encounter by which we may be invited by the author to come back with more of our own experiences and more of our own thoughts.

It doesn't matter if you write and read poorly—just do it with the confidence that they are both difficult activities, but not any more difficult then learning how to "like" certain things or write your own name. If you don't have confidence then you may have to do it through dumb faith, like you've learned to develop your personal tastes or draw your personalized fancy signature. Take your cue from Andy Warhol who was supposed to have said, "Don't cry. Work." Your daily work is not nothing. You are an inherently complex and valuable person who is able to test the pliability of both the material and conceptual worlds. This is what makes you and your students artists-in-residence.

Demystify the "labor = worth" paradigm

There is an anecdote told about Picasso which I heard from different teachers when I was an undergraduate in art school. It may or may not be true, but all these years I've been reluctant to verify its authenticity because—even if it weren't true—the reminder presented in the parable has been so useful to me.

The story goes that Picasso was due to have an exhibition at a gallery. He arrived to the installation of the show with nothing in his possession but a pile of paper and a pen. The gallerist—understandably—was puzzled by Picasso's empty hands and more so by his nonchalance. The gallerist was due to put on a show of new Picasso's. When a few hours passed, Picasso emerges from the back office with a pile of drawings that he had made that afternoon at the gallery. Incensed, the gallery owner starts berating Picasso about the breeching of their supposed agreement. He yells at Picasso that he was promised a show of "Picasso's" and that all he was getting was a

stack of drawings that "only took you a few
hours to make!" This legend ends with Picasso
ripping the drawings out of the gallerist hands
and storming out the door, exclaiming, "It took
me my whole life to make these!"

I think the moral of the story is that it's not always
easy to tell what goes into a manifested—or
outward—gesture. The thing we're looking at may
look insignificant. We may have even witnessed its
creation and therefore feel positive about how
insignificant or unworthy it is. But the complexity of
a lived life sometimes only offers us a few buds to
examine.

I've studied a lot of conceptual art and I've made a
lot of work through the permissions of conceptual
art, and I can actually guarantee that even the most
flippant looking gesture, isn't. Even if the artist
admits to the flippancy, think about what that artist
needs to know in order to make such a gesture. To
have a semblance of peace in the *Teacher as Artist-
in-Residence* posture we must believe that there is
complexity in the things we're witnessing even when
the evidence is pointing in the opposite direction.
This assumption will also help us to understand—
even our seemingly inconsequential moves—as
impactful.

This mode-of-operation is more of a mental
exercise than a hard truth. Of course, there are
thousands—if not millions—of art works that

exist because certain specialized individuals have developed refined skills that enable them to be one of a tiny handful of humans who can bring that thing to fruition. Think of those objects or performances you would readily put in the "art" category; there's no denying that those things are art. But labor equaling worth in an artwork is no longer the standard. You've seen it too, an artwork that is overly-labored— maybe even skilled—and yet communicates nothing.

Alternatively, a whole batch of artworks that are more hotly contested in terms of whether or not they are artworks to begin with can be very informative to a person attempting to be a *Teacher as Artist-in-Residence* specializing in minor, seemingly insignificant gestures. This is a polarized philosophical discourse that has ardent proponents on both sides of the argument. The Teacher as Artist-in-Residence doesn't need to take a side. I can appreciate skilled craftmanship or traditionalist artworks, while still learning from the permissions allowed to me through an engagement with the discourse about labor equaling worth in art. Although the debate about what is art is important, for conceptual artists the most important thing about the debate is that it is happening. The fact that the discourse exist is—in and of itself—a material that conceptual artists work with.

Understand relationships as part of a wider (sometimes slower) contemporary art discourse

I have already hinted to how the durational aspects of teaching are on par with something that happens in conceptual art. To put a finer point on it, there is a vibrant—albeit inconsistent—type of work that is currently being made in the contemporary art world and it follows a post-post-modern tendency to not only take liberties with the past, but rather to do something in the world that is *for* the world— even if the art dies in the process. There's no consensus on a name, but if you look up Socially Engaged Art you'll be able to find all its siblings: participatory art, civically engaged art, dialogic art, relational aesthetics, etc. This is a type of practice that takes its cues from conceptual art to think through relationships, public works and services, and participation as the main aspects of the works. No summary of the problems that arise with Socially Engaged Art can be attempted here, but it might be sufficient enough to say that teaching—and more poignantly, being in a school—provides an antidote to the savior mentality that sometimes permeates Socially Engaged Art because it is so real and undeniable.

The conceptual artist in the school might begin to see how impactful their participation in this large—fully situated—social enterprise really is.

They may begin to realize that teaching is truly a social practice that comes with ready needs, ready politics and power dynamics, ready diversity and communities, ready desire for change and discovery, ready social engagement, and—again, through the permissions of conceptual art—ready opportunities for making/enacting something radical and rarely seen before. Artists who are interested in Socially Engaged Art should become teachers.

The question for *Teacher as Artist-in-Residence* is how can the relationships one engages in as a teacher be collaborative to the point of artistic invention, while always considering the ethical implications of making art with or out of such an intimate situation? I don't have all the answers for that since I'm still in the thick of it, but I have learned that one key factor is *slowness*. Slowness and all the other things that we've been doing for generations to navigate and forge our relationalities: Training ourselves to be patient; reminding ourselves to be kind; trying not to be jealous *or* braggadocios; being humble and lifting others up even when it might be easier to put them down; teaching ourselves to not be selfish even though our instinct and education make selflessness feel counterintuitive; developing a longer fuse (or maybe even extinguishing it); stopping ourselves from accumulating "receipts"; not finding entertainment in the misfortunes of others, but always looking for the truth; being protective and trusting of others; above all things staying hopeful and persevering.

Know that everyone is brimming with expertise

You—the teacher—are, as explained in the opening parts of this lecture, an expert of the highest caliber; but so is everyone else you encounter. *Teacher as Artist-in-Residence* tries to create platforms for the expertise of others. When a student raises their hand or contributes to a discussion, it is a serious thing—even if it is made in the form of a joke. Parents know things. Other teachers and even administrators know things and the things that they know aren't only the things that lead to the efficiencies of schooling. Strangers know lots of things and they are everywhere. They sit and stand next to us on a regular basis. I'm not being totally Pollyannaish here. Do your vetting, but then get to the business of sharing expertise.

Work in the realms of the invisible, the dematerial, the deskilled, the indeterminate and the durational

You already do this, just accentuate it. Don't accentuate it for the sake of showing it, although there's nothing wrong with that; accentuate what you do in these realms for the sake of materiality. Once you see or acknowledge what you are doing then you can test its pliability.

If I could summarize what I mean here, I would just remind us that the teacher works in the realm of the invisible because what they do on a daily basis is both immeasurable and unspectacular to the average observer; the teacher then also works through the dematerial because they are actively seeking to bracket the everyday as a means to demonstrate expertise and therefore the ability to make creative contributions. All of this is done with a more generous notion of what is a legitimate contribution and who gets to make it. This whole work ends up being unpredictable and long, sometimes lifelong. It may in the end be so blurred into daily life that it might not be art at all. This then may be the most radical form of expression to ever exist.

Trust accumulation and duration

This one is lifted from *Teacher as Conceptual Artist* and also referenced briefly a moment ago when I was talking about reading and writing. It's based on the premise that a singular thing, say a sticky-note, may not have much of a presence; but 365 of those notes, placed in a grid really packs a punch. The Teacher as Artist-in-Residence needs to trust that a consistent methodology, even with small, incremental moves eventually gathers a certain kind of force. It's mere physics.

Make iteratively and incrementally, constantly

On the same note of accumulation listed on the previous mode-of-operation, a *Teacher as Artist-in-*

Residence needs to make iteratively (meaning multiple attempts of the same thing), incrementally (meaning a little at a time) and do this work constantly. Always be doing it. We live in a very important moment for this type of horizontalized creative practice. Without a doubt everyone in this room has a device—maybe a phone—and that device is a potable artist studio. What can't you do on that phone? It's an all-knowing library, a camera, an audio recorder, a jukebox, a map, a drawing table, a note taker, a photo editor, a sound effects machine, a television AND cinema, a social network, a map, an exercise trainer, and so many more things that can help an artist to make their work.

You're carrying your studio around in your pocket and this reality converts the whole world into your studio. Only death can stop you from making. Maybe.

Document everything
Given your portable studio there really is no reason to not document everything, even things that you don't think need to be documented. You can always go back and edit your documentation to tell the story you want to tell. However, if you didn't document it, then you'll have very little to work with. I'm not a particularly good generator of content, but if I have a pile of content that I've collected, I can edit it to form something that is representative of the work I've done.

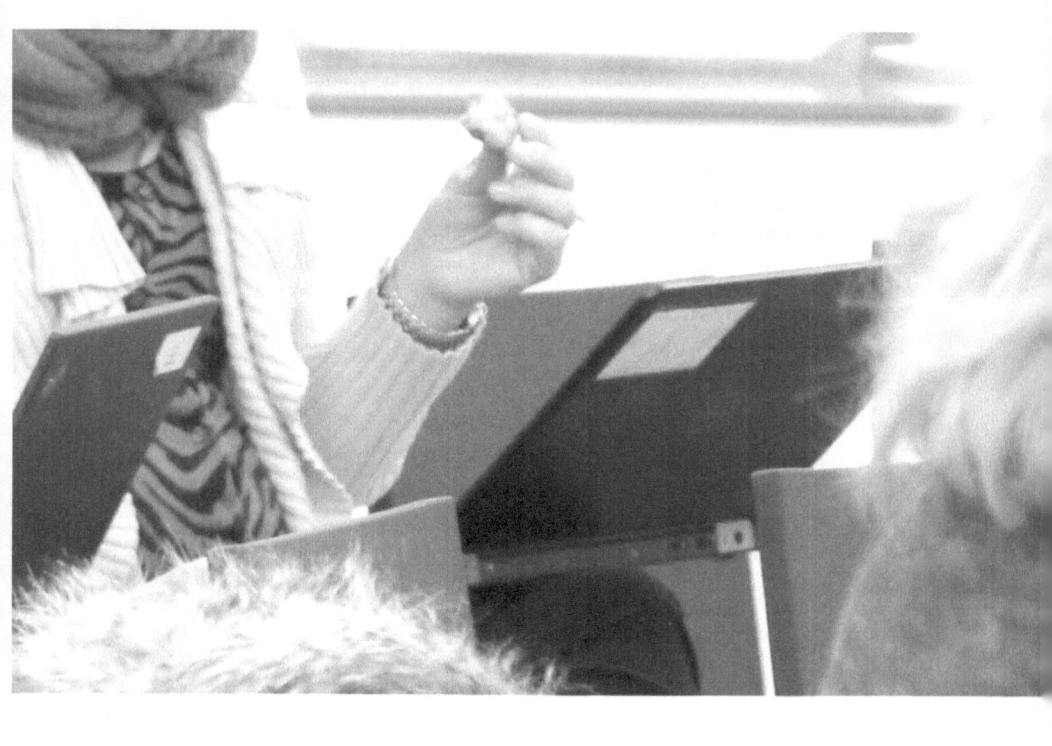

[2]

THE MATERIALITY OF SCHOOLS AND SCHOOLING
How is the everydayness of school a pliable thing?

Writing prompt for Chapter 2

~

Material is something that gives resistance, but it can be made pliable with the right tools, gestures, thoughts or force.

List things that could be considered material at your school or in the schooling you are near.

You might accentuate a quality in order to see it better. For example, if something is boring or tedious, you might lean into that.

Remember, you're not a trickster. You're not a troublemaker. You just want to pay attention closely. What has potential?

all these things can
change
yearly/monthly/weekl
y/daily/hourly/moment
to moment:

art supplies
black felt tip pens
crayons, pencils, and
scissors left on the
floor at the end of the
day
paper
non-white cardstock
pencils...pencils...penc
ils...and did I say
pencils?
lost pencils
pencil sharpeners
popsicle sticks
modeling clay
painting with
watercolors
Mixing red, blue,
yellow and then
some...ta-da!
microscopes
small binder clips in
the large binder clip
container

small milk cartons in
the cafeteria
supply budget
shoddy materials
lack of materials
recycled materials
trash
composting

books
dictionaries
bi-lingual dictionaries
practice books
textbooks
the books in the
library
computers
iPads
internet
technology
phones
P.A. systems
SMARTboards
SMARTBoard
Activities
supplemental videos
outside of the school's
firewall
copier
copy codes
paper allotment

printing
mailboxes
mailboxes as
shredders
sign-in book for staff
the water level on the
Keurig machine
paper towel supply

animals
animal containers
dog in the classroom
farm animals
(chickens)
freeze dried bees
living things
stuffed animals
the trash can named
"Chuck"
nonliving things

classroom furniture
all-in-one desks
bookshelves
bulletin boards
chairs, pillows,
rockers, floor for
seating options
class decorations

classroom desk
arrangement
rug placement within
classroom space
cubbies
jammed lockers
lighting
sound
music playlists to play
in the classroom
scent within classroom
spaces
new crayon smell
the smells constantly
change
adjustable thermostat
in each classroom
tables
time out/break chairs
whiteboards
wobble stools
writing surfaces for
students and teachers
seating charts

backpacks
comfortable shoes
hair color of students
dress code for students
dress code for staff
school uniforms

mulch in your shoes
my dress/apparel
staff ID photos
team jersey vest
wear jeans, I'm an
adult
wearing jackets
outdoors or not

Do I have to teach
inside my classroom?
Do all students have to
eat lunch together in
the cafeteria?
the outside space can
change
bus issues
bathrooms
adult bathroom lines
amount of pee on the
kindergarten bathroom
floors
cafeteria
cafeteria stage
classroom libraries
closets
educator spaces
field space
garden
gymnasium
hallways

cello player in the
hallway
office space
outdoor space
parking lots
patio space
room assignments for
teachers
storage
teacher workroom
the school building
the tool shed

ceilings
concrete floors to draw
on
cozy reading corners
doors
floors
garden beds
light fixtures
locked doors
lockers
picnic tables
railings
school bus seats
stairs
statues
the building pillars
wall space - negative
and positive

windows

anchor charts
content planning
curriculum
cultural norms
data spreadsheets
duty schedules
evaluations
email
grades & grading
graphic organizers
hall passes
homework
journals
lesson plans
lists
organization
presentations
projects
school websites
slides
special education
during art class
STEAM activities
sex education
strategic thinking
student readiness
subjects
testing
unit plans

virtual checklists.
Where are they,
because no one can
find them in virtual
reality?
weekly video
messages from the
superintendent
worksheets
yearly literary
publication

black top activity
games
icebreakers
indoor recess
make a comedy
P.E. equipment
parachute equipment
playground equipment
rules on the
playground
using sticks at recess
sports
school concerts
fire drills
tornado drills

free breakfast
iced tea for teachers

my lunch/snacks
nibbling on the
popcorn on the floor
nice cafeteria with
good food, coffee, and
diet soda for teachers
nice salad for teachers
salad bar
Starbucks on site

Backwards Day
Bike, Walk, and Roll
to School Day
birthday celebrations
school book fair
Dot Day
Field Day
Halloween
holiday parties
meatless Mondays
Picture Day
Red Ribbon Week
(drug awareness)
sick days
snow days
end of the year
shortened by unused
snow days
end-of-year
celebrations

"good mornings"
morning
announcements
morning duty
arrival times
8am meetings on
Mondays
beginning the day with
music and dance
routines and
procedures
time - not being ruled
by it but molding it to
your purpose
all academic times
bell schedule
class periods
collaborative time
computer time for
school learning
conferencing with
students for writing
more time for read-
alouds
taking movement
breaks
lunch
longer recess
snack time
the non-luxury of
being able to go to the

bathroom and leave
the room whenever
you want
length of lessons does
not follow proposed
plans for the day
distributing materials
to teachers or students
writing the date on the
board
lining up in the
hallway
Pledge of Allegiance
and mean it
moving through the
hallways alone or with
a class
the rules change
sometimes I don't care
if the rules change
dismissal
ending the day with
silent dismissal
after school activities
after school
procedures for
students
overtime
retirement

bus duty
chaperone field trips

recess duty

Each semester I begin
again.
Life is short, so are
first graders.
Every three years, it's
a whole new group of
kids.
Your colleagues
change, too.
Education by nature
must be spontaneous
and fluid.
I need to stop
changing the plan.
The plan can change.
You only need three
good plans.
While we have
standards to teach and
curriculum to follow,
the beauty of teaching
is finding the best way
to engage your
students so that they
love learning.

allowing students to
guide the math

introduction with
number talks
allowing students to
lead the learning
through their interests
and expertise
allowing students to
share thinking on
smartboard for class to
discuss
how I teach red words
reading with students
allowing them to
choose the book and
genre and topic

academic choice
meeting
boring teacher
meetings
Collaborative
Learning Teams
(CLTs)
committee meeting
conferences
cooperative learning
curricular therapy
fewer meetings
Individual Education
Plans (IEPs)
interim reports

lesson planning
more meaningful
meetings
my planning period
observations
Parent Teacher
Conferences
priority of curricular
concepts and social
concepts
professional
development
PTA events
required planning
meetings where no
planning gets done
role as a wellness
ambassador
sharing out data and
information
SMART Goal
soliciting / providing
feedback between
administrators and
staff
staff social activities
Standards of Learning
(SOLs)
support from our
administrators
team meetings to
discuss curriculum

change and student
needs
union meetings
unrequired planning
meetings where
teachers get
everything done
yearly evaluations by
administrators /
follow-up conference

the people
administrators
affinity groups
assistant principal
birthday committee
(oy)
blended families
instant families
communication with
other schools
communication with
the outside world
communities of
families
counselors that pull
students based upon
teacher referral only to
find out student
requires more

intervention than
initially thought
co-workers
crossing guard
involved parents
parent communication
principal
respectful students
students with behavior
problems
substitutes
talking and talking and
talking students
team members
volunteers

The most pliable
materials you'll
encounter in school,
besides, well, yourself,
are the students you
teach. They flex, they
grow, they shrink, they
bend, they push back,
they expand, they
evolve, they challenge,
they inspire.

Accordingly, my 25
most pliable materials
are as follows...

		acceptance of what's
1.	Sammy-Bam	normal
2.	Tuck Tuck	adapt
3.	So So	age
4.	Felicity-Lou	allowing students to
5.	Spiderman	share thoughts and
6.	Blue	ideas
7.	Tessa Monfressa	attitude
		balance
8.	Aya Mombaya	be grateful
9.	Irie-Lou	be kind
10.	Gabe-o-saurus Rex	be kind
		behavioral alternatives
11.	TJ	being present
12.	T	breathing
13.	Danester	burn-out
14.	Annika-bo-bannika	capability to risk mistake
15.	Jacy-mon-fracy	care
		classroom bloopers
16.	E	concern
17.	Gav	conformity
18.	Cammy Bam	conversations
19.	Gray	conversations about
20.	Jack Jack	belief
21.	Little Levi	coy comments from
22.	Henry...	students laid out as
23.	Pat	genuine questions
24.	Mac-kay-kay	which is actually an
25.	Oh-liv-e-ah	invitation to
		engage...To respond

or not to respond?
That is the question.
Dance like Elaine
Benes!
death
determination
distractions
eliminate foolishness
endless questions
energy-level
everyone deserves to
be loved
expectations from
students
expectations of self
experience
fear
feeling alone
have compassion
home life
hugs
hunger
inconsistency
inequity
inflexibility
inspiration
joy
kid's smiles
language
laughter
lead by example
learn from others

length of teaching
light-bulb moments
listen
love of reading
model the behavior
moods
never-ending stories
nimble with numbers
old things can be
exciting again
openness
palpable fun
play
public persona
reading books
relationships
(colleagues and
students)
respond
Say "thank you" and
"I am sorry."
Say, "I made a
mistake, please forgive
me."
school spirit
secrets
sense of security
sense of space
share
sharing ideas
sharing of materials
sharing of space

show empathy
sing
Stop. Look. Listen
stress
student minds
students and teacher
laughing together in a
musical symphony of
pure joy
take turns
tears
the memories
the reflection
the talk
the teacher's will
the thoughts
the walk
trust
value others
vulnerability
weather
whispering rumors to
your friends
willing to do whatever
it takes
words shared in
confidence
work ethic

All of these come and
go with fluidity

throughout the
day. The crisis, and
recovery flow through
the room with
ease. Students come
in distraught and two
hours later laughing,
adolescence...

Let
the everyday building
begin.

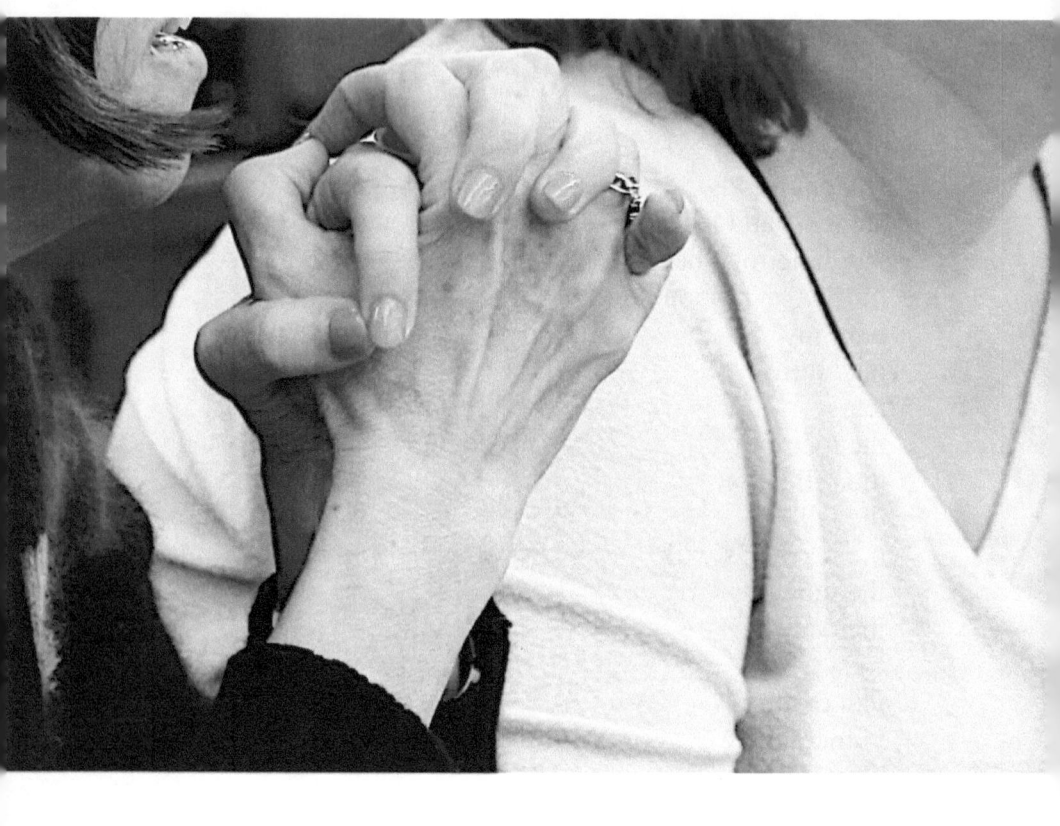

[3]

THE LITERATURE (TEXTUAL) REVIEW

What do we already know that opens up this way of working?

Writing prompt for Chapter 3

~

The literature review is resources,
bibliography, favorite quotes,
inspirational movies, songs, works of
theatre or dance. Artist or teachers
who we've seen do this work. Links to
websites, apps or downloads.

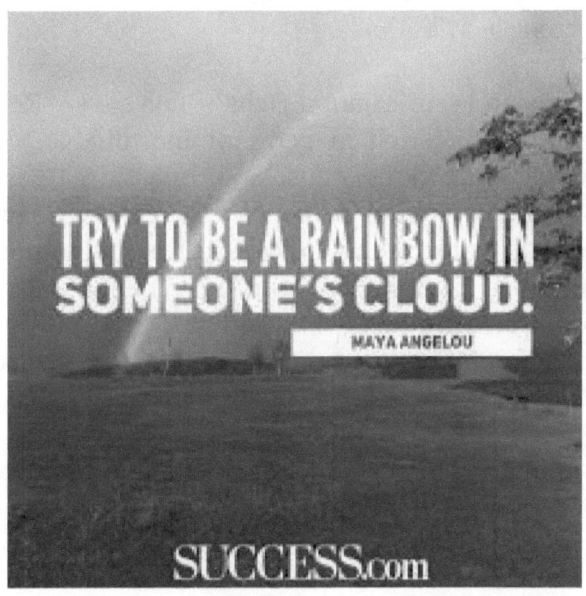

We delight in the beauty of the butterfly, but rarely admit the changes it has gone through to achieve that beauty. – Maya Angelou

I don't expect to find inspiration. It just of comes. Sometimes you step on a bug and you get inspired. – Iris Apfel

It is during our darkest moments that we must focus to see the light. – Aristotle

Running isn't just running. It's also frolicking, meandering, prancing, cavorting, sashaying, soaring, scurrying, dashing, sprinting, strutting, flying, leaping, skipping, kicking up our heels, and letting down our hair. – Kristin Armstrong in *Mile Markers*

The Persian Manifestation Baha'u'llah says, "Regard man as a mine rich in gems of inestimable value. Education can, alone, cause it to reveal its treasures and enable mankind to benefit therefrom." This is something I think about before each period to remind myself that each student is not a receptacle I'm to dump information into, but a mine I'm to pull gems from. My job is to help the students polish their own gems.

The moment where you doubt whether you can fly, you cease forever being able to do it. – J.M. Barrie, *Peter Pan*

Love the quick profit, the annual raise, vacation with pay. Want more of everything ready-made. Be afraid to know your neighbors and to die. And you will have a window in your head. Not even your future will be a mystery anymore. Your mind will be punched in a card and shut away in a little drawer. When they want you to buy something, they will call you. When they want you to die for profit, they will let you know. So, friends, every day do something that won't compute. Love the Lord. Love the world. Work for nothing. Take all that you have and be poor. Love someone who does not deserve it. Denounce the government and embrace the flag. Hope to live in that free republic for which it stands. Give your approval to all you cannot understand. Praise ignorance, for what man has not encountered he has not destroyed. Ask the questions that have no answers. Invest in the millennium. Plant sequoias. Say that your main crop is the forest that you did not plant, that you will not live to harvest. Say that the leaves are harvested when they have rotted into the mold. Call that profit. Prophesy such returns. Put your faith in the two inches of humus that will build under the trees every thousand years. Listen to carrion--put your ear close and hear the faint chattering of the songs that are to come. Expect the end of the world. Laugh. Laughter is immeasurable. Be joyful though you have considered all the facts. So long as women do not go cheap for power, please women more than men. Ask yourself: Will this satisfy a woman satisfied to bear a child? Will this disturb the sleep of a woman near to giving birth? Go with your love to the fields. Lie easy in the shade. Rest your head in her lap. Swear allegiance to what is nighest your thoughts. As soon as the generals and the politicos can predict the motions of your mind, lose it. Leave it as a sign to mark a false trail, the way you didn't go. Be like the fox who makes more tracks than necessary, some in the wrong direction. Practice resurrection. – Wendell Berry, *Mad Farmers Liberation Front*

Here is the world. Beautiful and terrible things will happen. Do not be afraid. – Frederick Buechner

I would maintain that thanks are the highest form of thought, and that gratitude is happiness doubled by wonder. – G. K. Chesterton

Never give up! – Winston Churchill

You can be scared and really ready. –
Daniellelaporte.com

You'll silently bloom,
Beautifully
In your own way.
– Dhiman

In order to destroy, we must create. – EE
Cummings

By being yourself, you put something wonderful in
the world that was not there before. – Edwin Elliot

Imagination is more important than knowledge.
Knowledge is limited. Imagination encircles the
world. – Albert Einstein

Logic will get you from A to B. Imagination will
take you everywhere. – Albert Einstein

Either write something worth reading or do
something worth reading about. – Benjamin Franklin

Tell me and I forget. Teach me and I remember.
Involve me and I learn. – Ben Franklin

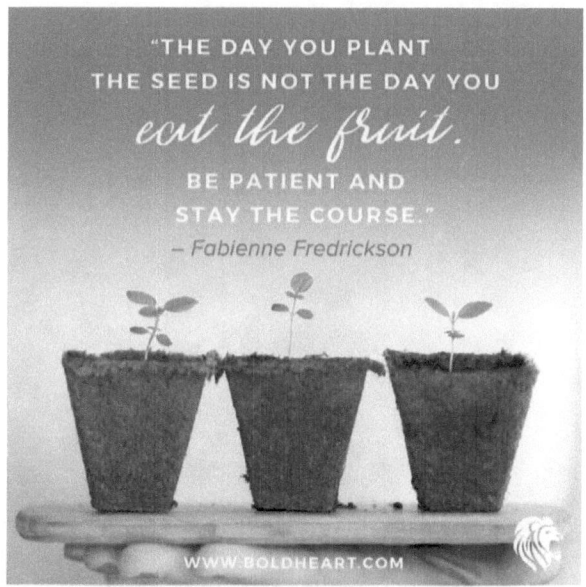

"THE DAY YOU PLANT THE SEED IS NOT THE DAY YOU *eat the fruit.* BE PATIENT AND STAY THE COURSE." – Fabienne Fredrickson

The beginnings of all human undertakings are untidy. – John Galsworthy

Be the change you wish to see in the world. – Gandhi

That's most of what we've got. We don't actually remember much of what happens. Instead, we get what we've rehearsed. If we fail to rehearse, the memory will fade. And if the memory isn't serving us, we can work to stop rehearsing it. Choosing what we rehearse is a way of choosing who we will become. – Seth Godin

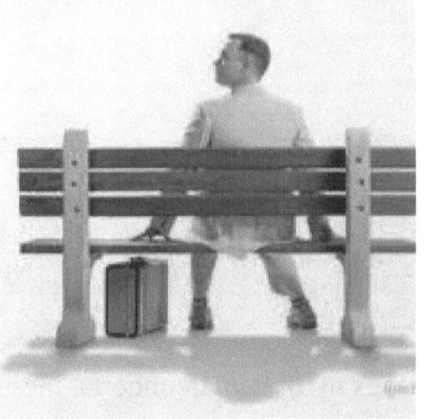

Mama always said life was
like a box of chocolates.
You never know what you're
gonna get. ~Forrest Gump

Think twice before you speak, because your words and influence will plant the seed of either success or failure in the mind of another. – Napoleon Hill

Waiting is an action. – Amy Imbody

Nothing that you haven't given away will really ever be yours. – CS Lewis

When you do something beautiful and nobody noticed, do not be sad. For the sun every morning is a beautiful spectacle and yet most of the audience still sleeps. – John Lennon

As we let our own light shine, we unconsciously give other people permission to do the same. – Nelson Mandela

We craft our hopes and dreams when we are given some mental space. Space creates desire and it's those desires that move us forward, let us create dreams, which in turn push us to create and act. – Medium Corporation

"What day is it?" asked Winnie the Pooh. "It's today," squeaked Piglet.
"My favorite day," said Pooh.
– A.A. Milne, *The Adventures of Winnie the Pooh*

If you don't write it down, I'll never remember. – my Mom

The greatest poem ever known
Is one all poets have outgrown:
The poetry, innate, untold,
Of being only four years old.

Still young enough to be a part
Of Nature's great impulsive heart,
Born comrade of bird, beast, and tree
And unselfconscious as the bee-

And yet with lovely reason skilled
Each day new paradise to build;
Elate explorer of each sense,
Without dismay, without pretense!

In your unstained transparent eyes
There is no conscience, no surprise:
Life's queer conundrums you accept,
Your strange divinity still kept.

Being, that now absorbs you, all
Harmonious, unit, integral,
Will shred into perplexing bits-
Oh, contradictions of the wits!

And Life, that sets all things in rhyme,
may make you poet, too, in time-
But there were days, O tender elf,
When you were Poetry itself!
– Christopher Morley, *To A Child*

The aliveness is in staying a verb. – Mark Nepo

An essential part of true listening is the discipline of
bracketing, the temporary give up or setting aside of
one's own prejudices, frames of reference and desires
so as to experience as far as possible the speaker's
world from the inside. – M. Scott Peck

Every child [and teacher!] is an artist. – Pablo
Picasso

Trust yourself, you know a lot. – Responsive
Classroom PD (a phrase to use with students)

Be patient toward all that is unsolved in your heart and try to love the questions themselves, like locked rooms and like books that are now written in a very foreign tongue. Do not now seek the answers, which cannot be given you because you would not be able to live them. And the point is, to live everything. Live the questions now. Perhaps you will then gradually, without noticing it, live along some distant day into the answer. – Rainer Maria Rilke

Creativity now is as important in education as literacy, and we should treat it with the same status. – Ken Robinson

Anyone who does anything to help a child in their life is a hero. – Fred Rogers

Discovering the truth about ourselves is a lifetime's work, but it's worth the effort. – Fred Rogers

No one can make you feel inferior without your consent. – Eleanor Roosevelt

When you reach the end of your rope, tie a knot in it and hang on. – Franklin D. Roosevelt

One crisis at a time. – Dwight Schrute from *The Office*

Somewhere along the path, running became the canvas upon which I documented my life. – Dangy Scott

Grande Flat White, please. – Liz Snead

Take chances. Make mistakes. Get messy! – The Frizz

Do I really look like a guy with a plan? – the Joker/me as teaching artist-in-residence

You keep using that word. I do not think it means what you think it means. – *The Princess Bride*

And though she be but little, she is fierce.

–Shakespeare

Don't ask yourself what the world needs. Ask yourself what makes you feel alive and then go do that. Because what the world needs is people who have come alive. – Howard Thurman

Trust the wait.
Embrace the uncertainty.
Enjoy the beauty of becoming.
When nothing is certain, anything is possible.
– unknown

We need to care less about whether our children are academically gifted and more about whether they sit with the lonely kid in the cafeteria. – unknown

You were my favorite hello and my hardest goodbye. – unknown

I'll be your mirror
Reflect what you are, in case you don't know
I'll be the wind, the rain and the sunset
The light on your door to show that you're home
When you think the night has seen your mind
That inside you're twisted and unkind
Let me stand to show that you are blind
Please put down your hands
'Cause I see you
I find it hard to believe you don't know
The beauty you are
But if you don't let me be your eyes
A hand to your darkness, so you won't be afraid
When you think the night has seen your mind
That inside you're twisted and unkind
Let me stand to show that you are blind
Please put down your hands
'Cause I see you
I'll be your mirror
I'll be your mirror
I'll be your mirror
I'll be your mirror
I'll be your mirror

– Velvet Underground, *I'll be Your Mirror*

The more complex the behavior demanded by a
situation and the less direct its solution, the greater
the importance of (inner) speech. – Vygotsky (1978)

Printed my name on the back of a leaf and watched it
float away.... – Wilco, *Via Chicago*

You are braver than you believe, stronger than you
seem, and smarter than you think. – Winnie the Pooh

Above all, trust in the slow work of God.
We are quite naturally impatient in everything
to reach the end without delay.
We should like to skip the intermediate stages.
We are impatient of being on the way to
something unknown, something new.
And yet it is the law of all progress
that it is made by passing through
some stages of instability—
and that it may take a very long time.

And so I think it is with you;
your ideas mature gradually – let them grow,
let them shape themselves, without undue haste.
Don't try to force them on,
as though you could be today what time
(that is to say, grace and circumstances
acting on your own good will)
will make of you tomorrow.

Only God could say what this new spirit

gradually forming within you will be.
Give Our Lord the benefit of believing
that his hand is leading you,
and accept the anxiety of feeling yourself
in suspense and incomplete.
 – Pierre Teilhard de Chardin

And regardless of what else you put on, wear love. –
Colossians 3:14a

I will give you a new heart and put a new spirit in
you. – Ezekiel 36:26

For God is not unjust so as to overlook your work and
the love that you have shown for his name in serving
the saints, as you still do. And we desire each one of
you to show the same earnestness to have the full
assurance of hope until the end, so that you may not be
sluggish, but imitators of those who through faith and
patience inherit the promises. – Hebrews 6:10-12

In returning and rest you shall be saved; in quietness
and in trust shall be your strength. – Isaiah 30:15

He has told you, O man, what is good; and what does
the Lord require of you but to do justice, and to love
kindness, and to walk humbly with your
God? – Micah 6:8

Let your gentleness be evident to all. –Philippians
4:5

Trust in the Lord with all your heart and lean not unto your own understanding. In all your ways acknowledge Him and He will direct your path. – Proverbs 3:5-6

Be still and know that I am God. – Psalm

God, grant me the serenity to accept the things I cannot change, the courage to change the things I can, and the wisdom to know the difference. – Psalm

My favorite quotes from movies or shows that make me laugh:

> "You're a fake and a phony and I wish I never laid eyes on you."

> "If Jill Goodacre gives you mangled animal carcass…you take it!"

> "How much for a rib? How much for a sip of coke?"

> "I'm difficult." "But in a good way."

> "I'm going to be forty." "When?" "Someday."

> "What did I say?" "You said, "What are you doing afta?"

"She doesn't mind double chins."

"Married"

"Pivot!"

"They don't know that we know that they know we know."

All's well that ends well.

Art and music are an "apapacho" to the soul.

Be kind to everyone for you never know the battles they are fighting.

Be kind more often than is required.

Be able to forgive people.

Blog, Blog, blog about your work...e-very-day! I have been writing about my practice for the past 11 years and the accumulation of all my work, right there, accessible, on social media, can easily get me a job anywhere in the country. Use that camera to take pics of your work and tweet daily what you do. Learn the power of hashtags. My twitter is @cutelisart and blog is www.cutelisart.blogspot.com.

Climb every mountain.

Consult colleagues who teach a different grade or subject than you do. Look through their lens at a topic you teach.

Go to national/state conferences. You need to connect with others who are just as passionate to get you to dream bigger.

Learn how to take good photos of your kids working.

My mother always told me to kill them with kindness. Anytime that someone is being difficult or giving me a hard time, I always go out of my way to show them extreme kindness.

Never cut what can be untied.

One day at a time.

People will either choke your dreams or stretch your vision.

Ramé (n): something that is both chaotic and joyful at the same time

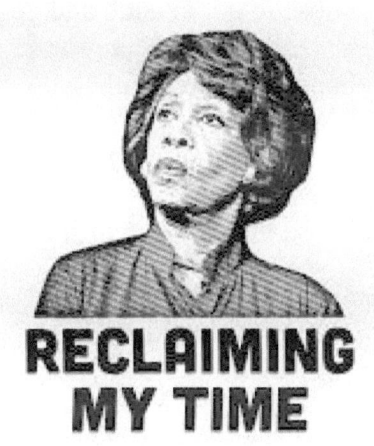

RECLAIMING MY TIME

Sometimes when I need inspiration, I default to my own online library and pool of resources. Statements. Screenshots. Messages. Posts. Comments. Sharing with you, what works for me.

The 12 Choices
(from HappyTeacherRevolution.com)

1. I choose to be happy.

2. I choose to disconnect and detach with love.

3. I choose to be mindful.

4. I choose to make time for sleep.

5. I choose to get outside and get moving.

6. I choose to be grateful.

7. I choose what to overlook.

8. I choose the battles worth fighting.

9. I choose what to do next time and what to stop doing.

10.   I choose to enjoy the relationships that matter.

11.   I choose to schedule and prioritize what really matters.

12.   No matter how the school year started, I choose to finish well.

The Arbinger Institute has a lovely methodology for behavior: behavior is driven by mindset; change mindset, change behavior. Sometimes, the educator has to be willing to be humble enough to consider themselves as contributing to a problem.
How are you contributing to a classroom management problem? To a student who is not performing? To a behavioral issue? How are you contributing to the success or failure of a lesson?

The grass is always greener on the other side.

The human brain is an anticipation machine, and 'making future' is the most important thing it does.

The Washington Post, I still look at it every day, no matter how brief.

They may forget what you said, but they will always remember how you made them feel.

Tikkun Olam: a Jewish concept defined by acts of kindness to perfect or repair the world

The Diving Bell and the Butterfly by Jean-Dominique Bauby

The World According to Humphrey by Betty G. Birney

the biographies of Eleanor Roosevelt, Abraham Lincoln, and the apostle Paul

Goodnight Moon by Margaret Wise Brown

Those Shoes by Maribeth Boelts

Bon Appétit magazine

A Little Princess by Frances Hodgson Burnett

The Secret Garden by Frances Hodgson Burnett

The Name Jar by Yangsook Choi

Recipes. My current favorite recipe book is *Dinner* by Melissa Clark, but often they're something I see and want to try.

I believe in the scientific notion that energy cannot be created or destroyed; that it only shifts forms and permeates all aspects of life. In literature, I've found this represented in the book *The Alchemist* by Paolo Coelho. His main character goes on an adventure of destiny. One of the powerful lessons is that when you want something, all the universe conspires in helping you achieve it.

The Miraculous Journey of Edward Tulane by Kate DiCamillo

The Little Prince by Antoine de Saint Exupéry: "One sees clearly only with the heart. Anything essential is invisible to the eye." This is extremely important to me in my life and my relationships and as a teacher.

How to Think Like Leonardo da Vinci by Michael J. Gelb

Without a shadow of a doubt, every educator needs to read *Linchpin* by Seth Godin. It teaches you how to harness your ideas and make them matter in any system. Seth Godin's ideas are revolutionary. Drop everything and go get his book. You are welcome. He also has an amazing blog.

Les Misérables by Victor Hugo

The Color of My Words by Lynn Joseph

"Mrs. Todd's Shortcut" in *Skeleton Crew* by Stephen King

Hooway for Wodney Wat by Helen Lester

The Invisible Boy by Trudy Ludwig

"I Am" poems inspired by *Where I'm From* by George Ella Lyon

One Hundred Years of Solitude by Gabriel García Márquez is one of my most valued literary works.

Winnie the Pooh by A.A. Milne

Making Thinking Visible by Karin Morrison, Mark Church, and Ron Ritchhart

Esperanza Rising by Pam Muñoz Ryan

In Light of India by Octavio Paz

When Dad's at Sea by Mindy L. Pelton

The Bell Jar by Sylvia Plath

His Dark Materials series by Phillip Pullman

Martin's Big Words: The Life of Dr. Martin Luther King by Doreen Rappaport

Reader's Digest, 1989-1996

The Next Step Forward in Guided Reading by Jan Richardson

Musicophilia: Tales of Music and the Brain by Oliver Sacks

Catcher in the Rye by J. D. Salinger

anything by David Sedaris

Where the Wild Things Are by Maurice Sendak

Seventeen, 1989-1992

East of Eden by John Steinbeck. I have read this book every year of my life for the past 29 years, and every year I come away with a new thought about it.

"The Teacher as Artist" by Warren Sylvester Smith in *The Journal of General Education*
Nudge: Improving Decisions About Health, Wealth, and Happiness by Richard H. Thaler

Educated: A Memoir by Tara Westover

Don't Let the Pigeon Drive the Bus! by Mo Willems

Proust and the Squid: The Story and Science of the Reading Brain by Maryanne Wolf

any song by Prince

Beethoven

Can't Stop the Feeling by Justin Timberlake

Celebration by Kool & the Gang

Children's songs to move my class

Chopin

Elvis Presley

Escape (The Piña Colada Song) by Rupert Holmes

Eye of the Tiger by Survivor

Hap Palmer is a children's musician with a great website on how to incorporate his songs into curriculum and activities. www.happalmer.com

Harry Belafonte

It Is Well With My Soul by Audrey Assad

Moana playlist

Music is an inspiration and medicine for the soul.

music that inspires me to create dance

Música Latina makes everything better

My Favorite Things by Julie Andrews, because there is always something positive to find in your day.

"No Good Deed" from *Wicked*

Queen

Scarlatti

Smile by Nat King Cole as performed in the movie *My Girl* by Vada's mom.

songs by The National. I love their New Yorker type poetry/lyrics.

The Chicken Dance by Werner Thomas

The Masterplan by Oasis

"The Power of Yet" as performed by Janelle Monae on *Sesame Street*

The Three Tenors first CD compilation

Zombie by The Cranberries

There is a moment in the movie *Amistad* that I saw in theatres, at an incredibly impressionable 16 years of age, which has never left me. John Quincy Adams is speaking to Cinque, preparing him for the ordeal which he is about to endure and the stakes of the whole court case. Cinque has this unshakable faith. It was the first time I learned that there are moments where people are speaking to each other, but are not really in the same conversation, a point I've been sensitive to since. Yet, there's a moment where Cinque tells Adams they won't be going into the courtroom alone. Adams notes that they have the best lawyer possible and righteousness on their side. Cinque responds, "I meant my ancestors. I will call into the past, far back to the beginning of time, and beg them to come and help me at the judgment. I will reach back and draw them into me. And they must come, for at this moment, I am the whole reason they have existed at all." There is a historical lineage to that statement that shifted my whole life and how I considered the reality of mortality, history, the interconnectedness of everything and energy.

Clueless. My favorite movie. I love how stupid these really smart kids were. It's just a reminder that not everyone has common sense. Never assume what other people know.

Coco

Dead Poets Society is an inspiration for the life well lived as a passionate teacher.

Galaxy Quest is a perfect movie.

Midsommar

Steel Magnolias

The Red Balloon

The Sound of Music is my film of all time.

For me, *The Sound of Music* represents the resilience of the human spirit.

Paw Patrol is an excellent RELA teaching tool for 6th graders. One 30-minute episode packs a plot, decision making, conflict, character development, antagonists, protagonists, climax, rising action, falling action, and whenever Captain Turbot is involved, puns and alliteration. Teamwork can mean that not every pup is used for every mission, which involves detachment, but sometimes a pup may be needed later, which involves readiness.

PBS *Nature* series because, my dog loves to watch it and it reminds me how beautiful the world is.

Doubt

El Ingenioso Hidalgo Don Quijote de la Mancha! by Miguel de Cervantes Saavedra has been a great inspiration for me in my life, in doing the best I can, to dream the impossible dream, and reach for the stars. In fact, when I graduated as a teacher, we as a class chose the song "The Impossible Dream," because it deeply inspired all of us to strive to be the best of our abilities, not only as teachers, but as individuals.

Hamilton

Jersey Boys

Les Misérables

Motherhood Out Loud is a play composed of a series of monologues and vignettes about the varying experiences, expectations and aspects of motherhood. I had the opportunity to perform as a member of its cast recently, and it is a literary reminder to me that the more specific something is, the more universal it can become.

musical theatre

Phantom of the Opera

Red

RENT

Spring Awakening

Swan Lake ballet

Wicked

Alfie Kohn video *The Schools Our Children Deserve: Rescuing Learning from Grades, Tests, and "Data"*

Calm an app

Facebook teaching groups are great resource.

Google Images is great for clipart, activity pages, photos, etc.

http://artsedge.kennedy-center.org/educators.aspx

https://www.nationalgeographic.org/education/professional-development/educator-certification

https://www.nga.gov/education/teachers/teacher-institute.html

LifeLab.org

No matter what your job offers, have your own personal Google Drive to save ALL of your unit slideshows. Then share them with your school drive.

Oprah's *Super Soul Sunday* podcast is the best inspiration out there for new books/authors/ideas.

PhotoGrid is an awesome photo collage app that allows you to add words, borders, and watermarks.

Pinterest is an endless source of inspiration.

Project Zero

Ron Berger's video *Austin's Butterfly: Building Excellence in Student Work*

Sir Ken Robinson's Ted Talk *Do Schools Kill Creativity?*

teacherswithasenseofhumor.com (It's a Facebook page too.)

The Smithsonian Learning Lab

Tony Robbins podcast

www.pecentral.org

www.teacher2teacher.education

Chris Stylz Bacon as musician and artist

Jamin Carter's cut paper with student narratives (illustrations of climatic scenes)

Carmen Lomas Garza's cut paper, metal cutouts, paintings and artwork

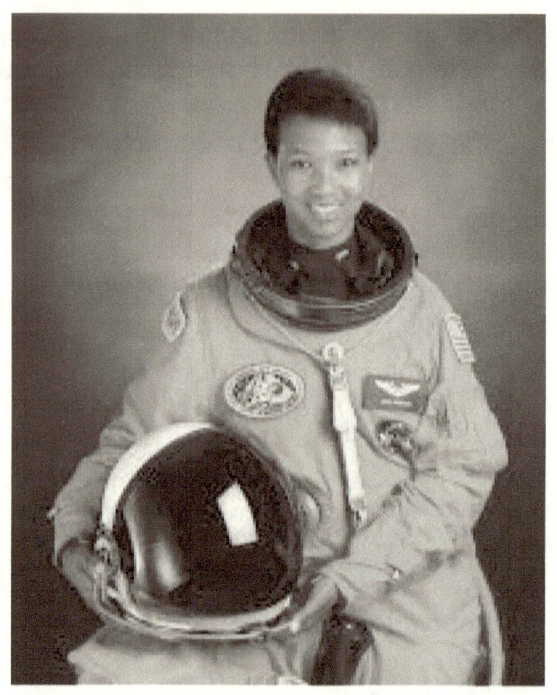

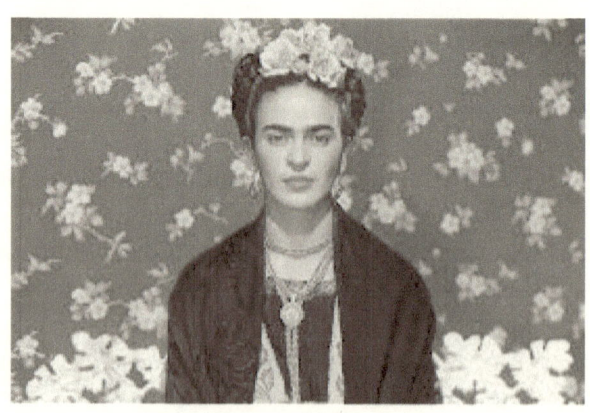

John Steinbeck

Kennedy Center Teacher Workshops

my mother who became a chemist after she was denied admission into medical school because she was a woman

my mother who is a teacher

My son with special needs is an inspiration and endless lab for me to try different strategies before implementing them in the classroom.

Parkland Teens who protest gun violence

Smithsonian Workshops

Teacher Night at the museums

Titus Kaphar's layered portraits recreated with self-portraits

animals - all of them with the exception of the mosquito but it makes feel a little guilty not to like the mosquito so I will try

art and theater to integrate curriculum

Cooking inspires me to take my time and wait patiently to see the result I expect from my students, just like I do in the kitchen waiting for a wonderful risotto to be perfect.

crayons

diving in the warm waters of the ocean with my snorkel and following a fish to see where it goes

Every educator needs to become a runner. Running has helped me stay sane and balanced. Schools are places where emotions often run high.

gardening

Japanese Flower arranging (Ikebana)

Japanese woodblock prints

Lake Michigan

my bicycle

my passport

my sketchbook, which I add to daily

new shoes in the spring or new running shoes any time of year

secret stash of chocolate

the art at the Louvre

the barn I grew up in the smell and the feel of it and all of the places we created to play and learn and live

the complexity and simplicity of language and communication

the perfect fondue in Switzerland at the lake in Lucerne

the water. I grew up on an estuary and always look for that space.

travel and new cultures

Veggie juicing every other day has kept me healthy for over 7 years now. I am going on my 8th year of no antibiotics.

Windjamming

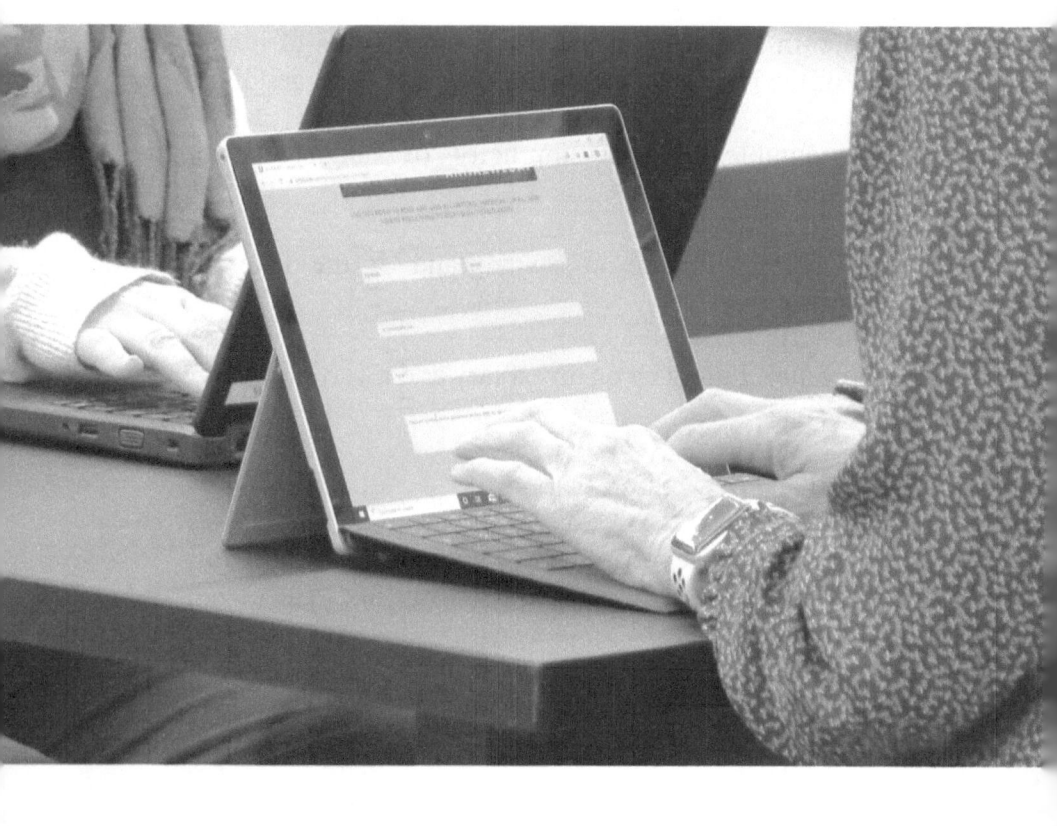

[4]

FRAMEWORKS AND POSSIBILITIES

If we had it all—or absolutely nothing—what would we do?

Writing prompt for Chapter 4

~

If we had it all—or nothing at all—
what would we do? With our
students, with our colleagues, with
our communities, by ourselves, in our
homes, in our dreams, in our
classrooms? What are the possibilities
if there were no limitations of
permissions, money, time, energy,
resources, labor, collaboration?

What are the possibilities if you have
nothing? What is left? Time,
relationships, love, survival, the body,
thoughts, our voice, earth…

It is really hard to dream of a teaching world without constraints or limitations...

It would have many more counselors, therapists, social workers, and psychologists. Class sizes would be smaller. There would be a closet with unlimited supplies for students who might need them (clothes, food, books, pencils, etc.). Students with disabilities would have the support they needed to succeed whether that be extra adults, e-books, communication devices, or supportive peers. The pressure of statewide testing would be removed so that the pace of instruction could slow down if it needed to and concepts could be covered in more depth than breadth.

In those moments where something "clicks," when risks are being taken and momentum of creativity is flowing, I would not look at the clock, stop it, and line up because we have to get the kids to the next place.

Teachers would be allowed the freedom to do what is best for their students that particular year rather than required to push curriculum that is too challenging and causing frustration.

I would let the kids explore and guide the lessons and figure out the lesson in their learning.

If I had it all, I'd have everyone work on individual projects and toss out the state standards. I'd have a classroom assistant to wash the brushes and deal with materials management. I'd never grade, because it doesn't matter really.

I would spend time working with students to help them create work that is complex, beautiful, and authentic.

My class would create an art installation and invite outside guests to view the pieces.

I would have creative freedom to stray from the county's pacing guide as long as learning was happening and wave good-bye to standardized testing.

I would put social-emotional learning on the same plan as "academic learning."

I would have movement breaks (games, dances, improv, etc.) throughout the day. I would spend 10-15 minutes of each 60-90-minute period doing this so the other 45-50 minutes could be more productive.

I would insist that colleagues understand that fun and learning can co-exist.

We'd go outside more than once a day. We'd play in rain and snow.

I would take my class on a camping trip. I would love to

watch them explore the wide open with each other. I would let them build a basecamp, a temporary home, make their own dinner, pitch their own tents. Classrooms are this amazing space of community and appreciation of individuals. I think this gets lost sometimes. I think taking a moment to escape to a piece of untouched nature would just be such a powerful exercise that would allow the kids to discover their own abilities and appreciate those of their classmates.

In a teaching world without restraints, I would take my students on a field trip each week. We would be able to go around the world sampling the food, customs, meeting people. It would be immersive in the culture, experiencing the every day. I would have complete control of the curriculum.

I would take the students on international field trips to see all of the items and objects we were learning about.

I would take the lessons outdoors. Let the students learn through doing. For example, if we were learning about money, we would actually go shopping. If we wanted to learn about measuring, we would actually go to a construction site to help build.

I would take students to art museums and have classes there.

If I was still a second-grade teacher, I would take my kids to Mexico to see the Oyamel Forest in the winter to see the monarch butterflies. We would go back during the spring to see the butterflies leave the forest and head north!

I would have famous children's authors and illustrators come to my classroom and interact with the kids about how writing changed their lives. It would make a published author tangible to the students. They could ask questions and see how the author comes up with ideas

There would be a monthly book club for teachers to go to used book sales, thrift shops, etc. to shop for books together for their classroom libraries, especially to curate author studies for our students.

If I really had it all, I'd have a sunlit studio to do my own work in and enough time to explore every idea I think up.

If I had it all I would be volunteering in communities where they don't have access to arts education for kids and enrich their education.

I would try to solve the climate crisis.

A message of hope, love, and thanksgiving! The tree of life has so many branches and at the core of mine, celebrating others is a hidden treasure. Who knew my passion would manifest in taking those on a broader, experiential journey from the inside out? As I reflect back to look forward, the next year is baked with gratitude…keep walking!

I would hire people to get life
necessities at home done such as repairs, cleaning,
organizing etc. I would delve into my passions, spend
more time doing what I enjoy, and travel to
explore new places, people and cultures. I would fly
to other places to take part in special educational
opportunities. I would accomplish my goal of
writing a book with my sister about our father.
I would get a few burdens off my plate.

I would teach in sweatpants and slippers…maybe just
on Fridays for a special treat.
I'd have a never-ending stream of my favorite
vanilla decaf almond milk lattes on-hand.
I'd have an assistant!!!!!!!!!!!!!!!!!!!
I'd get paid TWICE as much.

If we had it all, there would be no more "teams"
within the school – no Environmental Team, no
Instructional Team.

Teachers could count time as "comp time" whenever
they have a doctor appointment or sick day.

The school would allow coverage for teachers so they
can observe their colleagues in action.

Parents would be taught how to parent.

Kindergarten would be kindergarten again, less testing more teaching.

If we could do anything, I'd make educators in charge of education. We already know what kids need to make them feel safe, be able to grow and learn, and do their best. Yet, we do not trust this knowledge. We allow non-educators to be in charge of our profession. TEACHING is the only profession where we do not have control of our own profession. Non-Educators control how education is run.

As a nation we have creativity and innovation, yet we are told those things do not count. We are told to make our education like the education of other countries. We need to make education for who we are. We are about arts, creativity, freedom, human connection, and hope. As a 20-year educator, I am tired of administrators nervously trying to toe the line, a line set by a fear-based system, whose primary interest is not our children, but mere control.

If I had it all I would begin with some of my like-minded colleagues to take the work we have already done in class and expand it across the curriculum in an art filled thematic semester. For example, the project "Take One Picture" involved a school in England where the entire school studied one painting. Each discipline made it theirs. Students wrote stories, created math problems, designed equipment, and replicated machinery found in the painting. If we had it all, songs would be learned and sung based on the time period of the painting. Games in PE would be played in a similar fashion. Food and clothing would be researched and recreated in Home Ec. The idea of 1000 students sharing a common experience of a work of art and learning how to view it though every conceivable lens of thought is inspiring. Then, we would take all of these efforts collectively and exhibit them in the National Gallery so our students would see their work professionally displayed. I would ask the curators to discuss how they displayed our artifacts and the importance of these works to our culture as a whole.

Teachers would never have to buy school supplies like pencil sharpeners, staplers, and indoor recess games for their students.

I would have easels, paint and supplies in the classroom.

Each classroom would come with a classroom library.

There would be a big comfy couch (or two) in the middle of the classroom and a variety of flexible seating.

My dream is to have a classroom that is spacious with areas devoted to the arts, science, math, technology, and a classroom library. I would have a HUGE closet full of resources or all kinds. I would love to have a variety of technology including a 3-D printer, a laptop per child, and anything new.

I'd design a school building to accommodate all needs and with room for growth. There would also be a large empty space accessible to all during indoor recess days or whole-class activities.

I would open up the school and classroom to the world. Schools would connect with each other from all over the world on lectures, lessons, projects, and collaboration. Coming to school would mean seeing your classmates in-person and online. The classrooms would have moving walls to create different spaces, opened, closed, and the freedom to change the shapes of the room to allow collaboration and inclusion.

If I could build my own school, there would be two or more levels. It would have a central atrium or courtyard with fruit bearing trees and a vegetable garden. The school would have an auditorium independent of the cafeteria. It would have flexible, stadium seating and proper AV materials, inclusive of a basic theatrical black box lighting system.

The school would have a dance studio, choral music space, instrumental band/orchestral space, two visual arts studios, one for technology and digital processes, and the other for more analog media, including pottery wheels and a kiln.

There would be a full-court gymnasium, with bleachers, AV equipment and shower facilities. There would be outdoor classroom spaces and a full soccer field with a running track.

Each classroom would have a one-stall restroom and a full sink. There would be multiple options for classroom seating. Teachers would "shop" from options based on seniority and availability. Classrooms would have flexible lighting, dimmers, SMARTboards, manipulative white boards and a wall unit for books, supplies, and materials. Educators would be able to teach lessons in different classrooms, to keep things fresh.

The halls would be thematic and change throughout the school year or monthly for Hispanic Heritage Month, Women's History Month, Black History Month, etc. Student work would be on display, but more than curricular work. It would demonstrate how students are being affected by external forces and would include poems, sculptures, paintings, etc.

Students should feel free to express themselves. The expressions can lead to more fruitful discussions. Students would have space for self-expression, thought, and discourse. To the best of the school's ability, we would remove the barriers to their learning.

The staff would be balanced by a network of mental health professionals, guidance counselors, and nurses. There would be several administrators, each with a different, but complementary purview. Educators would have an option, based on seniority, to loop with their students, but would need to commit to looping for the full tenure of the student cohort at the school.

The cafeteria would have true service with whole foods and multiple options. No student would be denied a meal. Any meals left over would be available for students to take home at the end of the day.

Until the age of 8 or so, students would just play. Mostly outside. Sometimes together. Sometimes alone. There would be no formalization of this just time each day spent outside experimenting with the world.

After this, for a few years, ages 8 to 12 or so, every child would be placed in a cohort of 7 to 10 students from around the world. They would be matched roughly in age and language perhaps, but not in anything else. These 7 to 10 students would have two teachers who would be with them for at least a year, maybe more. During the course of the year, the teachers and the students would select three to four major areas of study. These major areas of study would then trigger the curriculum for the year. For example, if a student was really into the Vikings and another student was really into renewable energy, and the teacher was really into plate tectonics, then a study would commence in Iceland. The students and teachers would meet online for a period of weeks to gain some supplementary information about the topics. The cohort and the teachers would then travel to Iceland to study Vikings, geothermal energy, and tectonic plates. After this trip (which would last as long as needed within reason), the cohort would select their next area of study. Maybe one student is really into bats and another student is into festivals and how humans connect over tradition, and another student is really into varieties of the English language, then a trip to Trinidad would happen. Lather, rinse, repeat until a year of school is done.

At a particular age, puberty most likely, children would leave their cohorts and would no longer travel, but would instead move away from their homes to live in nature and would engage in fairly mundane and repetitive tasks. This would be so that they could spend a lot of time getting to know each other and playing out / trying out various roles in groups to see what works best for them. All health precautions (to ward off disease and pregnancy) would be given so that maximum experimentation could happen. After a few years of this, students would return home.

So, around the age of 15, children return home (if they are ready) and begin to engage in the practice of connection. Now that they have gotten to see how the world works and how relationships work, they will have the experiences to see how they are part of it and can make decisions to be involved. School is now left up to the student to create. They will connect with members of their community who can mentor them in their areas of interest. If a student is interested in knowing more about what it means to become a lawyer, they will find a lawyer who will take them on for as long as both parties are interested.

All of these experiences will be documented using blockchain technology. Potential employers would examine the blocks to see if the person had the right mix of experiences to move into the next phase of the job or into the next phase of education.

The real dream is to not only see yourself as an artist-in-residence, but to see your students through that lens as well (and eventually have them fully internalize the role). Model for your students all the best artistic habits of mind and open yourself up to be amazed by what they take in and bounce back.

Actually, there has to be limitations or there would not be the ideal of no limitations. Limitless money, time, energy, know-how, etc. would never lend itself to anything final as a product. Even with the concept of duration, a feeling of accomplishment comes from knowing that a person did the best they could and contributed to the whole. The joy of doing is working within the constraints to overcome them in showing what can be accomplished given those parameters. If I picked one thing to be limitless, it would be commitment.

If I had it all, I wouldn't use it all. Less is more, simple is beautiful, and I would continue trying to have a quiet balance.

[5]
A TEACHER AS ARTIST-IN-RESIDENCE THINKS ABOUT...

What do thirty-three artist-in-residence think about in 2019 and how is this the impetus of all the work we make, be it pedagogical, philosophical, ethical or creative?

Writing prompt for Chapter 5.

~

What does a Teacher as Artist-in-
Residence think about?

Remember that you are the expert. If
this is true then what is important to
you? Make a list of essential things
that motivate your work. How does
your work as an Artist-in-Residence at
your school help you to work through
those things which matter to you?

A teacher as artist-in-residence thinks about the students. What are their needs? What do they know? What do they like? What do they like to do? Do they like making a mess? Do they prefer music, painting, drawing, acting, dancing, photography, cutting, gluing, or modeling?

I think about how students, even those in elementary school, are just little people. Their ideas, interests, hobbies, fears, likes, dislikes, passions, grumpy moods, and bursts of excitement should be honored in the same way we honor fellow adults.

I think about kids, especially little kids, with their joy and hope and creativity and view of the world. It is really inspirational.

A teacher as artist-in-residence thinks about instilling a love of life-long learning in students, respect for what has come before and what can and will come after, joy in the process, knowing that they make a difference everyday whether good or bad. Each day is a new opportunity to grow. And they passionately look forward to vacations or time off!

I think about how to challenge students to dig inside themselves and express what they never even thought about.

I think about the feeling of resonance from your vocal cavities down to your toes when that one pitch feels just right. Can I create even a single moment where my students feel something similar, when their abilities give them that "tingle" of something good?

I think about how students have vast knowledge in them, and part of my job is to figure out how to allow that knowledge to flow out.

I think about how effortlessly creative and wildly imaginative my students are at any given moment.

I think about how much potential each child has, but how little nuisances get in their way.

Am I finding the gift(s) in each child?

I think about spotlighting the WHOLE child.

Can I have students be teacher/expert for a day? Could I mix up the learning and allow students to share their own expertise on topics? What if I had students create their own museums of items special to them that they collect?

When it is time for students to "show what they know," why can't they decide how to share what they have learned? There are so many possibilities: a PowerPoint, leading a class, a collage, sculpture, painting, a poem, a script, an original song, sitting down with me and talking, a hands-on demonstration, a Letter to the Editor, a flash mob. I think about how it's difficult to oversee and manage, but it's worth the work.

How can I reach my students in ways that go beyond the typical methods? How can my students demonstrate their knowledge in ways that best work for them?

What are the ultimate skills I want the students to walk away with?
How do I make a lesson impactful in a short amount of time?
How can I make it impactful for children?

Why does this matter?
What is the bigger picture?
How does it connect to the world?
What is the purpose of what I am doing?

What is the lowest common denominator of this lesson?
How will I know if the students understood the lesson?
How do I keep the students engaged in an activity?
What can I do to help this child learn and access the classroom experiences?
Why is this child trying to get my attention?

How do I engage all students while learning a new language?
How can I integrate art into language acquisition?
Why are language learners held to the same standards as other learners when experts know it takes up to 7-11 years to acquire a second language?

How can I integrate the arts into my curriculum?
How can I incorporate music and art into class?
Where can I find good visual references for my students?
How can I change the way everyday objects are viewed?
What is my art? What materials do I use?
What materials do we need for class?
What to do????

Where I can put things so that we have more surface area to work on?
Where did I put the things that were on the counter, now that I need them?

Will my project be accepted by students and perhaps admin?
How will parents respond/react to children's work?
Who in the community could semi-involuntarily volunteer for my next classroom collaboration?
Why don't I have enough time to do my number one job, which is to think and create and collaborate with other teachers for my classroom instruction/delivery?
Why aren't there any classroom teachers or retired classroom teachers on our School Board?
Why is Virginia an at-will state?

How do I make time to meet with the Art/Music/Movements Specialists in my school?
How can I best showcase my students' most creative accomplishments?
How can I infuse a creative mindset into my colleagues and/or administration?

Am I acting in a way that honors what I teach my students? So many times, I hear teachers talk about flexibility, open mindsets, kindness towards others. I often think about how powerful we would be if we acted in the way that we told our students to act.

I think about teaching kindness, empathy, integrity, patience, humor and modeling each.

I think about how powerful it is to share your life story with students. Telling students about your life as a person, not just a teacher, helps them connect with you.

I think about how I can share my own art making as a way to inspire students to make art at home.

How can I lay the foundation for being a good friend?

I think about teaching sensitivities and that it is okay to have different opinions or different anything.

Every single day in the classroom as a teacher has taught me far more than I ever learned (read retained) as a student in a classroom.

When something is irritating to me, am I questioning why, or just ignoring the unpleasant situation? If it is the latter, why?

Is my breathing calm, centered, purposeful?

How can I pay it forward?

Am I having fun while teaching?

Am I working with intention or just working?

Can I walk out of school and be proud of what we did, but leave it there so at home I have something of myself left for my family?

I think about the desire to do good work, to make things a little bit better than they were before (but then who is say what is better). I think about the best thought ever: Timshel! ("Thou mayest" from *East of Eden*).

To live, love, and laugh using the power of my passion in pursuit of purpose to life's greatest treasures. I think about serving people in every capacity. I think about the duty to help others achieve and the gift of empowerment. I think about how a concentrated and mobilized effort in small parts makes a huge difference. I think about how to celebrate victories along the way.

On purpose. Ask yourself from time to time, what statement are you making? Does it help you, or does it hurt you? Try to stay relevant in who you are and/or what you do. Eliminate content and images that do not add value to your purpose, your plan, or your personality. In other words, make it plain. Say more, with less. Is perception the reality? Just ask.

Every day, I get caught looking at my front view, my side by side view, and occasionally in my rear view—and I see the exact same person looking at me—my daily and my weekend crush—*Driving Ms. Tami.* "Where to next?"

I think about being part of the world and knowing that your movements matter and that it is all connected.

I think about being separate from the rest of the world and knowing that what you do isn't such a big deal. No permanent damage will be done.

I think about how teaching is not a platform to have power over other people.

I think about how progress can be slow, and I try to tell myself that it's okay.

I think about how to make my classroom a safe environment for everyone to feel comfortable to try new things and make mistakes.

I think about building a classroom and community within that classroom that allows movement and talking and collaboration and creative writing and drawing.

A teacher as an artist-in-residence thinks about making things fun for themselves.

I challenge myself to do new and maybe uncomfortable things for the sake of my class.

I think about changing and challenging the status-quo.

I think outside of the box.

I think about how to strategically ask for forgiveness rather than permission.

I think about the standards-based spin I can give my principal for spending an entire day playing outside in the dirt.

I think about taking risks. It's scary, but so worth it.

I think about doing something different that nobody else does. What makes you different?

I think about how unhelpful it is to have an inflexible mind.

I think about creativity, purpose, drive, individuality, and building confidence.

I think about more than just black and white. I think about lots of color.

A teacher as an artist-in-residence thinks about projecting confidence even if they don't feel confident.

I think about how to make sure the rules are followed are just enough to unleash the creative potential a person or a medium can handle.

I think about ways to break the mold.

A teacher as artist-in-residence thinks about doing the most conventional thing unconventionally.

A teacher as artist-in-residence talks, curses, and sings to herself.

I think about the cost benefit analysis of buying frozen worms on Amazon.
I think about multi-media.
I think about thinking.
I think about butterflies.
I think about teaching dance as part of the culture of Hispanic countries.
I think about becoming a well of ideas.
I think about how I hate waking up so damn early.

I think about finding time to walk the dog, because I get my best ideas when walking the dog. I also get great ideas in the shower, but I don't think about that.

When I am at the theatre, reading a book, at an art gallery, or walking down the street what am I seeing? How is this relating to my life and experiences?

A teacher as artist-in-residence thinks about how to show off the work students have done where it will NOT invite viewers to say it's cute. CUTE is an insult in most instances. If you can't see beyond the fuzzies I have failed.

I think about letting students know the goal is not perfection but practice.
I think about teaching that there is no such thing as perfect.
I think about how to put process over product...
while still somehow pulling together a kick-
@ss product.

If I need inspiration, so do my students.

I answer questions with more questions.

I think about doing stuff that excites and avoiding the rest.
I think about how much I care, and that maybe I care too much.
I think about how wonderful it is to share the burden with someone at work.
I think about sharing expertise.
I think about students reading books that allow creative thinking without telling the students WHAT they are supposed to learn from the book.

I think about how the trash at school does not actually get recycled, and how messed up that is that we lie to kids.

I think about how a recycled egg carton would make
a great palette for a painting unit, but don't want to
constantly carry trash around.
I think about getting more supplies while spending as
little money as possible.

A teacher as artist-in-residence thinks about how
they can provide quality substitutes when they take a
personal day.

I think about whether or not kids who see me sneak a
bite from my breakfast actually ate breakfast
themselves.

I think about lunch, except when I didn't eat
breakfast. Then I think about breakfast. After lunch I
wish I had chocolate in my desk, but usually there is
none.

I think about documenting life's most amazing
moments, every day!

I think about having a place to be and being needed
in that place.

I think about how my job is never done.

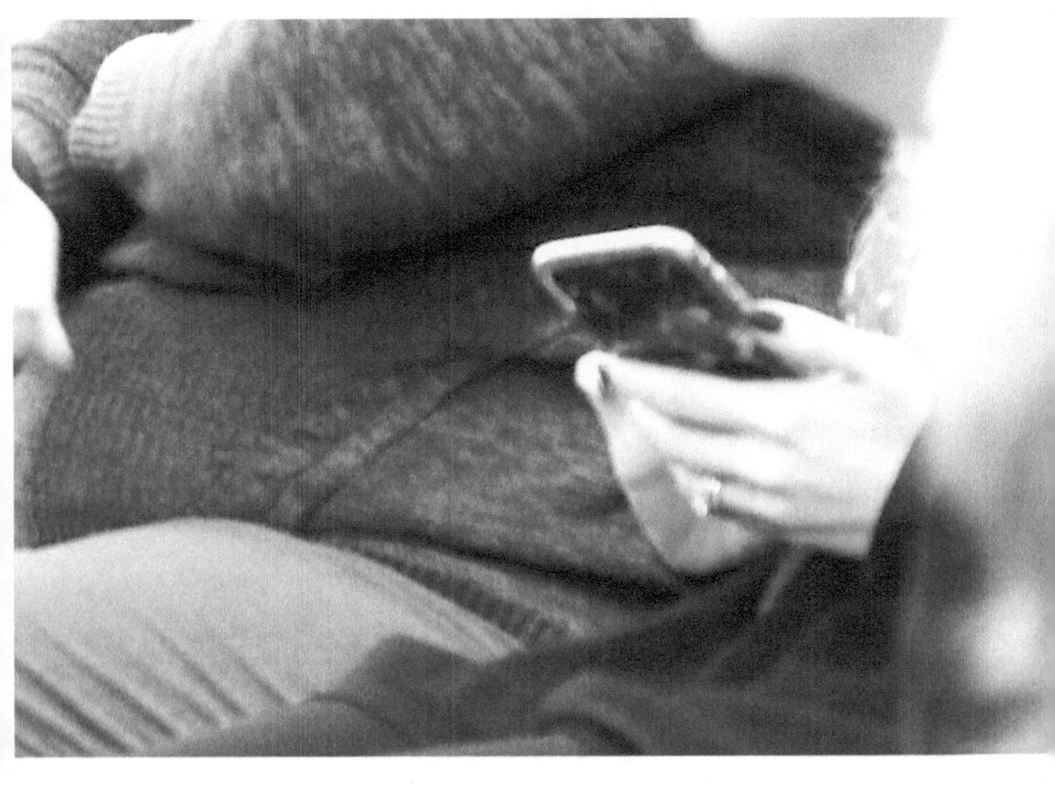

[6]
TIPS FOR TEACHERS AS ARTIST-IN-RESIDENCE

Writing prompt for Chapter 6

~

How might you encourage others to
see themselves as the experts in their
space?

Listen, observe, perceive, feel.

Know what you are going to do that day.

Don't think what worked last year will work this year.

When the lesson is going south, morph it into something else.

Forgive yourself if the lesson planned isn't the lesson provided in the period of time. Know that you are giving the people the best of you in the moment; you are in a safe space to breathe.

Don't be afraid to completely scrap your lesson plan.

Consider how you contribute to all aspects of your classroom.

Don't personalize reactions or results.

Never take it personally, unless it is good, then always take it personally.

Don't judge the outcome; evaluate the process.

Think about making meaning.

Think multi-sensory.

Art and music are as essential to your students' future as math and reading.

Before you tell a student to stop doing something, ask yourself if stopping their behavior is beneficial to them or if it is just beneficial to you. If it is the later, try to just wait.

Always when you call a student's home, word the complaint as "I need your support with this." When in doubt, assume all parents love their kids and want to help.

Give students permission to advocate for themselves.

Teach your students the benefits of mindfulness.

Listen to the students.

Allow your students to play. It fosters collaboration and communication.

Allow students to be students, and allow yourself to be a kid at heart from time to time. Remember who you were at this age.

To create bonds, share your personal experience with students and ask them to share.

Artists are supposed to break rules.

Allow your students to be creative. Not all students are great writers, but their drawings could tell a story, a personal narrative, or be a nonfiction work.

Remember that you might be the only truly creative teacher they've had all day.

Make mistakes in front of your students. Let them watch you own your mistake and grow from it.

If the room is loud, whisper. Don't raise your voice.

Those classroom brown paper towels don't pick up water. Keep some rags on hand.

Write down what your students say and read it often.

Kids are hilarious. Find something to laugh at every day. Write down the funny stuff they say.

Discover student's interests and dive into them.

Don't over decorate. Leave space for student input.

Take a moment. Let the feeling pass and breathe.

You can always take a breath.

Never, never, never, never give up.

Never stop learning.

Do what you can for the day, and then let it go. You can come back to it tomorrow if you need to.

Don't sweat the small stuff.

Keep it simple.

Don't be afraid to work hard.

Let others see you laugh and cry.

Always smile at everyone you pass in the hallway including grownups and students.

Be yourself.

You are the expert. Everyone is an expert. Approach everyone with that premise.

You are the expert! Your residency is 180 days! Enjoy your one-person, immersive-experience show!

No matter what others tell you, you are worthwhile.

Each day is a chance to start over!

Be creative and don't be afraid to fail miserably.

Enough is usually not enough. Certainly, there is more in store. Creativity is endless.

Savor every perfectly imperfect day, remembering you always get the chance to try things all over again tomorrow.

Don't get so hung up on the carefully practiced routine you forget to try new things. Students are resilient and flexible. Your lesson plans should be too.

Change things even though you think they shouldn't be changed. Change things even though you are scared to change them.

Remember that you are an art teacher, you make art and you teach art.

Your days will never mirror each other.

Remember you MUST be flexible.

Embrace the mess.

Remember the goal is to make sure these young minds grow up to be functional human beings.

Enjoy your days and find humor in what you do.

Beware of all of the candy and cupcakes.

Stay fit. Exercise. Do not eat all of the food that shows up at school each day.

Chocolate and Kleenex (guard closely and always have a supply).

Drink LOTS of water.

Google questions.

Digital is great but trust analog solutions.

You are learning and growing, just like your students.

Know that what makes you human also makes kids human. The same considerations should be given to both.

Doing is learning, for you and for your students. Getting it right the first time isn't necessary for either of you. The process is necessary to learn.

If you are excited, the kids will be excited too.

If you are not having fun with your lessons, neither are your students!

Your students' executive function will only be as good as your own.

Trust yourself. Trust your intuition. Trust your ideas and abilities. I'll say it again: trust yourself.

Make time for yourself and your family.

You need ME time.

When you need a break, take it.

Give yourself a break. You cannot control much of what you will encounter, only how you react.

Please stay home if you are sick.

Get enough sleep, you can't fake it.

Remember to take care of your own personal health and well-being. It's okay to leave at the end of contract hours even if things aren't done.

You are capable!

Constantly grow and evolve.

Honesty will always be the best policy.

Be empathetic with your students.

Make it actionable.

Make it your own and stay the course on your journey!

Stand for pay equity.

You don't make enough money to be miserable.

Know your worth as a professional. Lawyers don't feel badly about charging hundreds of dollars per hour for their services.

Speak up in meetings in support of what your students need.

Talk in meetings. Be a part of the process. Don't be passive. Find a way to be there.

Don't be afraid of your principal.

Support your team members. Be there to listen when they need to vent. Be there to celebrate successes.

Find out the birthdays of staff members at school and give them a birthday sticker on their special day.

Be grateful for what you have.

Teaching rocks!

Have fun!!! Be creative and take risks!

Never stop having fun.

Make teaching fun for me.

Sing and dance.

Giggle...at least every now and then.

Laugh (a lot).

Tell lots of jokes.

Always say please and thank you.

Say yes.

Make a mess.

Share.

Read.

Be kind.

Collaborate.

Listen.

Count your steps.

Don´t be so hard on yourself.

Laugh at yourself.

Don't take yourself seriously.

Be confident.

Have faith in yourself.

Do not underestimate yourself.

Do not compare yourself to other teachers, especially those teachers that you think are awesome.

Be easy on yourself. Give yourself credit.

This too shall pass.

Try again.

Stay soft.

Be vulnerable.

Be fearless and human.

Abolish perfectionism.

Be generous.

Help others.

Write down questions you have and put them away for a few days. There's something about giving someone else advice that seems easy. Walk away from your question and give yourself advice. You're an expert on your own students!

Trust your gut. You know your students best.

Stop doubting yourself. You know this.

There are only pauses, not endings.

Keep the notes, cards, emails, and any communication that is positive, always.

Positive and negative attention-seeking behaviors have one thing in common: they are trying to seek your attention. Figure out what they are asking/what they need.

When working with English Language Learners in a Reading, English, Language Arts context remove the language barrier altogether when introducing new text. Use images to start a dialogue, then add the related text. Now that we see how the painter or sculptor used tools, what tools did this author use?

Feel free to move schools. There is so much to learn from other staff and teachers that are not from the same community you are working in now.

When you're no longer passionate, find a new job.

Disney employees are called Cast Members because every aspect of the guest experience is part of the show. Sometimes, you need to play a role.

No matter what you do and who you work for, always consider yourself as self-employed, no matter where you are. Work as if no one was there to watch, grade, or evaluate it. But in fact, you are watching. Create work that makes you proud. No one else matters.

As long as no one gets hurt (too seriously), no one is going to mind what you do. Just in case, always have a supply of band aids.

Vent to colleagues on difficult days.

Do not let that angry person write that email.

Know who the wise ones are and have them read your controversial email before you send it.

Share your accomplishments with colleagues.

Find your cheerleader and be one for someone, too.

Surround yourself with other teachers who inspire you.

Compliment colleagues on a daily basis (on a personal level, or something about their classroom, or their students' behavior...).

Bring in a surprise box or coffee or some treats every once in a while, and leave it near the staff sign-in book or in the staff lounge. (If this is a financial burden, find a colleague or two to do this with).

Teamwork will make you work smarter, not harder.

Do not become "that" teacher that compares schedules.

Everyone works JUST as hard as you do, trust that and move on.

Fail forward and remember that life is ultimately all about transformative struggle.

Walk by faith, not by sight.

Question your initial assumptions, always.

Inspiration meets empowerment in every space we grace!

We are a blip on the students' radar. The kids are going to have so many other teachers and life experiences.

Your job as an educator is to prepare the feast for the child. You cannot force them to eat or help them metabolize.

Think of lessons as a buffet, not a sit-down meal. Offer way more than needed and hope students will take it and get what they need.

If your school district doesn't have a curriculum, and you are being forced to create it with your team with weak guidelines while given no time to plan and collaborate, don't blame yourself. It's not you!

Our job as educators is to remove the uncertainty for a child to feel successful as a writer.

There will be times when you feel like crying because you are so filled with love for your students. It usually happens to me when I'm reading to the students. Watch their faces when you read them stories.

Be extra nice to the secretaries and the custodians.

Your degree, title, or your administrative status does not earn you respect, you actually have to earn those with true work.

"Good mornings" go a long way.

Start where you are. Use what you've got. Do what you can. – Arthur Ashe

It's not you, it's the system.

Leadership does not JUST belong to the administration.

If I had no limitations, I would make all schools do two things and two things only teach how to lead and teach how to solve interesting and personally meaningful problems together. That is all school should do. (Inspired by Seth Godin's Linchpin).

If you stick with teaching, at the end of your career you will know you were part of something incredible and important...and you will be glad.

[7]
CONSIDERATIONS
As critical thinkers, what reservations, blind-spots, or unclarities might we have?

Writing prompt for Chapter 7

~

When 33 teachers reflect on the
potential limitations or difficulties that
would emerge if we started to think
of our school as material and of
ourselves as *Teachers as Artist-in-
Residence.*

There is a lot on your plate as a teacher and it can already feel overwhelming to balance the myriad of demands on your time and mental capacity. How can artistic projects and endeavors best be integrated into a busy professional life?

Playfulness begins with your attitude. Each lesson/show is a new audience. If you can watch a movie repeatedly and find something new, your students/audience can find something new in your lesson, or you. Children learn all sorts of skills with play. How can you turn what they need to learn into a game? Should you? They might have fun and learn something in the process.

I am an educator and practitioner serving the Washington, DC region and beyond. I am also a professional photographer capturing lifestyle portraits, special projects, meetings, and events. My mission and teaching practice consider active engagement with creative art expression, promoting mindfulness, social and emotional learning, and project-based applications for the whole person to connect life and the human journey. I consider cultivating growth mindsets and learning lifestyles by looking to people first and process second. I aspire to be an art therapist as my journey continues to bring out the best in others. #KeepGoingKeepGrowing and find me online @ tamiejohnson or by email CelebratingYou@tamiejohnson.com

School districts please buy a curriculum and provide it to your teachers. We are smart enough and experienced enough, surrounded by other experts and can adapt any curriculum, but we need a good starting point instead of reinventing the wheel from scratch every year.

Mandates from school system don't allow students the opportunity for creative growth.

Two big considerations in this age of "teaching to the test" are (1) What would parents say about this philosophy of teacher as artist-in-residence and doing things in the classroom that are not the norm? and (2) What would administrators say? How does all of this contribute to the bottom line of higher test scores?

Administration should support for teachers applying new strategies. This can be "messy." Support would allow teachers to try and incorporate new ideas.

School district administrators, stop asking us to enter data in three or more different places. That's not our job. Get an IT specialist to make a system in-house, oh yeah, it's called Blackboard.

Consider the end of year review. Before you go off on a wild tangent dragging your students behind you, think of some big sprawling educational jargon to throw at your immediate supervisor. They will be impressed.

Every school needs two school-based subs and two or more school psychologists. Having more reading specialists isn't going to help kids read, but maybe more school psychologists can help.

Many parents are not present. Their child is not their priority.

I'm very concerned about how parents are outsourcing parenting and not educating their children. Teachers are now spending more time teaching values and basic rules of socialization than their content.

Consider that your students are someone else's children.

Parents take your observations as observations, not as criticism of your parenting style. Our observations are there to help, not hurt. We don't want a child to have a learning difference, but we would not be doing our job if we did not tell parents.

I wish teachers would stop trying to regulate students. Students need to learn self-regulation by asking themselves, "What do I need to do to _____ (get ready to go outside, be prepared for science class, leave for the end of the day, etc.)."

Consider integrity.

Lack of imagination is a consideration.

I feel like I don't have enough time or resources to do the teaching I dream of doing.

Consider that there are going to be a ton of resources, but you don't have to do everything! Less is more at times.

It should be considered that teaching is a great profession. It is one that we should be lucky to be in. The problem is that it is a profession that is not as respected as it should be. I wonder, why is that?

You will know fairly quickly if this is the right job for you. Trust yourself to make that decision.

Let's just face it, we get in our own way. Are we afraid of what others will think? Are we caught up in what others want? Of course we are. We are human.

As difficult as it may be daily, after teaching for 40 years, I still find myself loving it and enjoying every day despite some problems with students with difficult behaviors. I find that students respond in a positive way when I teach songs and play the guitar for them.

No one is born knowing how to treat you. You need to teach others how to treat you, and this needs to happen every day.

If I cared what others thought of me, teaching would no longer be a joy for me. I close my door and do my best.

Education is a messy affair that is completely imperfect. In sixteen years, I have had amazing life affirming experiences and numerous heartbreaks. Every day I walk into that room with hope. I do not know what will become of my students. Some of those kiddos may go on to do amazing things and others may lose their way. All I can ask for is that while they were in my universe, they understood someone cared about them and wanted the world for them.

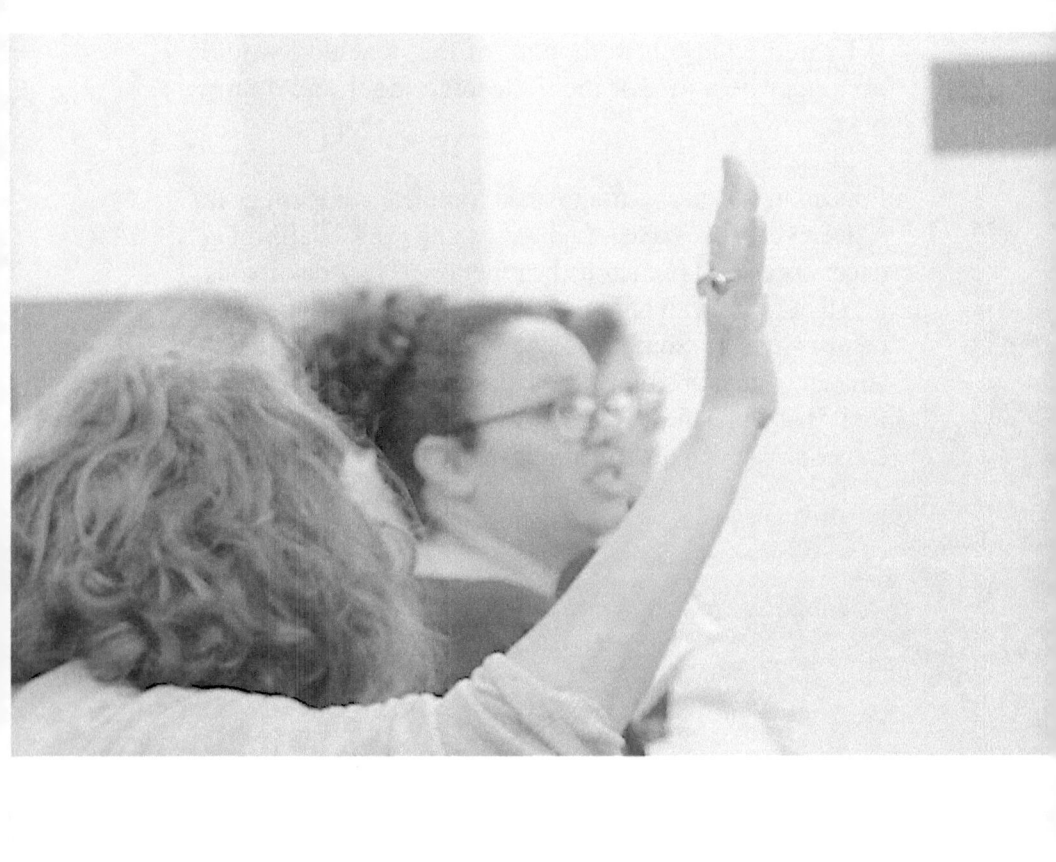

[8]
FURTHER READING

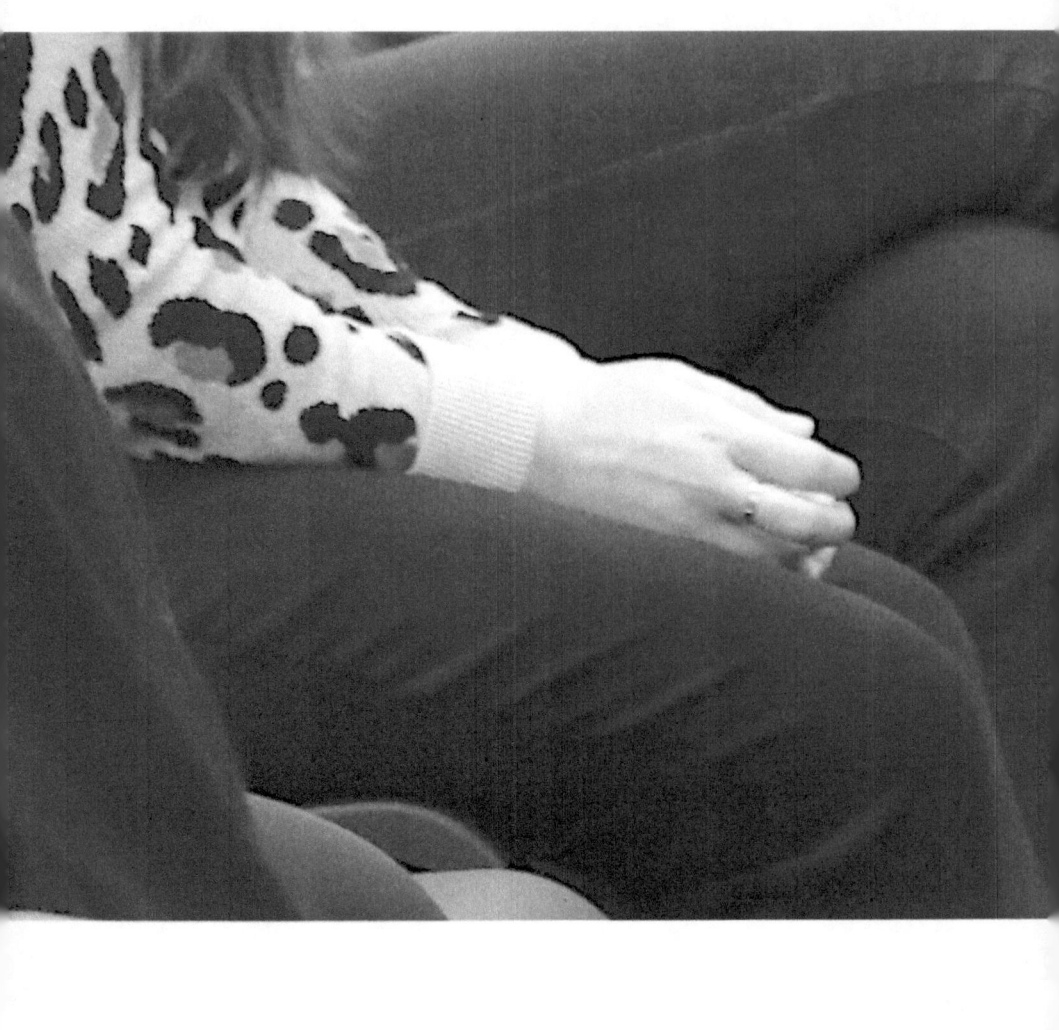

A list of everything that could be read related to the ideas presented in this book would be just as long—if not longer—than the book itself. I (Jorge Lucero) limited this *Further Reading* list to twenty-five texts that I've found repeatedly useful in thinking through and around *Teacher as Artist-in-Residence*, not just as an interesting idea, but as a continuous practice that I enact on a daily basis. On any given day, this list would probably look very different. As such, if you've made it this far in the book I would invite you to write to me in order to continue the conversation. You could write an email simply asking, "Hey Jorge, what are you looking at these days?". I will then respond with an addendum to this list of recommendations and we'll take it from there. I can be reached at jlucero@illinois.edu and mr.r.pup@gmail.com

Things to read, formatted in the APA style.

Allen, F. (Ed). (2011). *Education: Documents of Contemporary art.* Cambridge, MA: MIT Press.

Anderson, S. (1993). *In the spirit of Fluxus.* Minneapolis, MN: Walker Art Center.

Baldessari, J. (2013). *More than you wanted to know about John Baldessari: Volumes 1 & 2.* Zurich, Switzerland: JRP | Ringier.

Beuys, J. (2004). *What is art? Conversations with Joseph Beuys.* West Sussex, UK: Clairview Books.

Bloom, L. (2019). *Sol LeWitt: A Life of ideas.*
    Middleton, CT: Wesleyan University Press.

Bottoms, S.J. and Goulish, M. (Eds.). (2007). *Small*
    acts of repair: Performance, ecology, and Goat
    Island. New York: Routledge.

Bremmer, M., Heijnen, E., & Lucero, J. (2018).
    School as material - Modes of operation for
    teachers as conceptual artists. In S. Blom, M.
    Hermsen, F. Uiterwaal, B. Verveld (Eds.),
    Researching the arts (pp. 38-51). Amsterdam,
    NL: Amsterdam University of the Arts

Bruguera, T. and Bishop, C. (2020). *Tania Bruguera*
    in Conversation with Claire Bishop. Caracas,
    Venezuela: Fundacion Cisneros.

Camnitzer, L. (2007). *Conceptualism in Latin*
    American Art: Didactics of liberation. Austin,
    TX: University of Texas Press.

Camnitzer, L. and Alberro, A. (2014). *Luis*
    Camnitzer in conversation with Alexander
    Alberro. Caracas, Venezuela: Fundacion
    Cisneros.

Farver, J., Camnitzer, L. and Weiss, R. (Eds.).
    (1999). *Global Conceptualism: Points of origin,*
    1950-1980s. New York: Queens Museum of Art.

Friere, P. (2000). *Pedagogy of freedom: Ethics, democracy, and civic courage.* Lanham, MD: Rowman & Littlefield.

Goldie, P. and Schellekens, E. (2009). *Who's afraid of conceptual art?.* New York: Routledge.

Goulish, M. (2000). *39 Microlectures in proximity of performance.* New York: Routledge.

Heijnen, E. (2015). *Remixing the art curriculum: How Contemporary visual practices inspire authentic art education.* Retrieved on January 18, 2020 at http://www.emielheijnen.net/files/RTAC%20EM IELHEIJNEN.pdf

Heijnen, E. and Bremmer, M. (2020). *Wicked art assignments.* Amsterdam, Holland: Valiz.

Johnstone, S. (2008). *The Everyday: Documents of Contemporary art.* Cambridge, MA: MIT Press.

Kaprow, A. (2003). *Essays on the blurring of art and life.* Berkley, CA: University of California Press.

Kostelanetz, R. (Ed.). (1988/2003). *Conversing with Cage.* New York: Routledge.

Lippard, L.R. (1973/1997). *Six years: The dematerialization of the art object from 1966 to 1972.* Berkley, CA: University of California Press.

Ono, Y. (2000). *Grapefruit.* New York: Simon & Schuster.

Osborne, P. (2011). *Conceptual art: Themes & movements.* New York: Phaidon.

Rashkin, E. (2009). *The Stridentist Movement in Mexico: The Avant-Garde and Cultural Change in the 1920s.* Lanham, MD: Rowman & Littlefield.

Tognato, C. (2018). *Cultural agents reloaded: The legacy of Antenas Mockus.* Cambridge, MA: Harvard University Press.

Witkovsky, M. (Ed.). *Light years: Conceptual art and the photography, 1964-1977.* Chicago, IL: The Art Institute of Chicago.

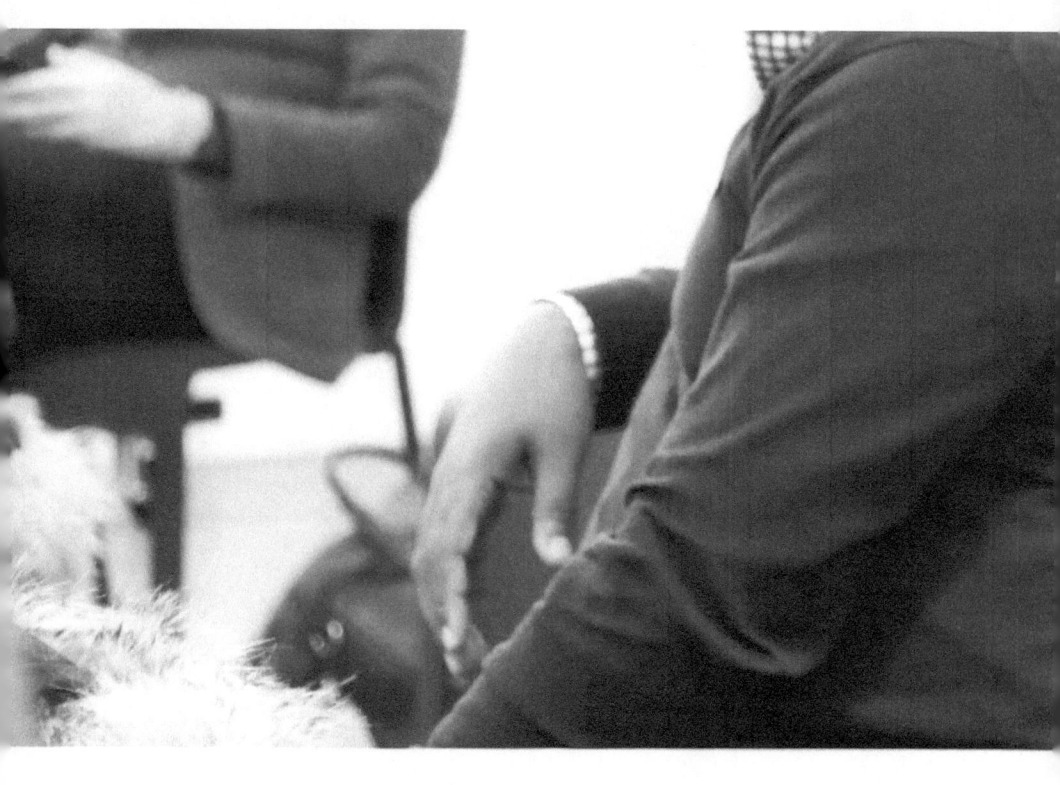

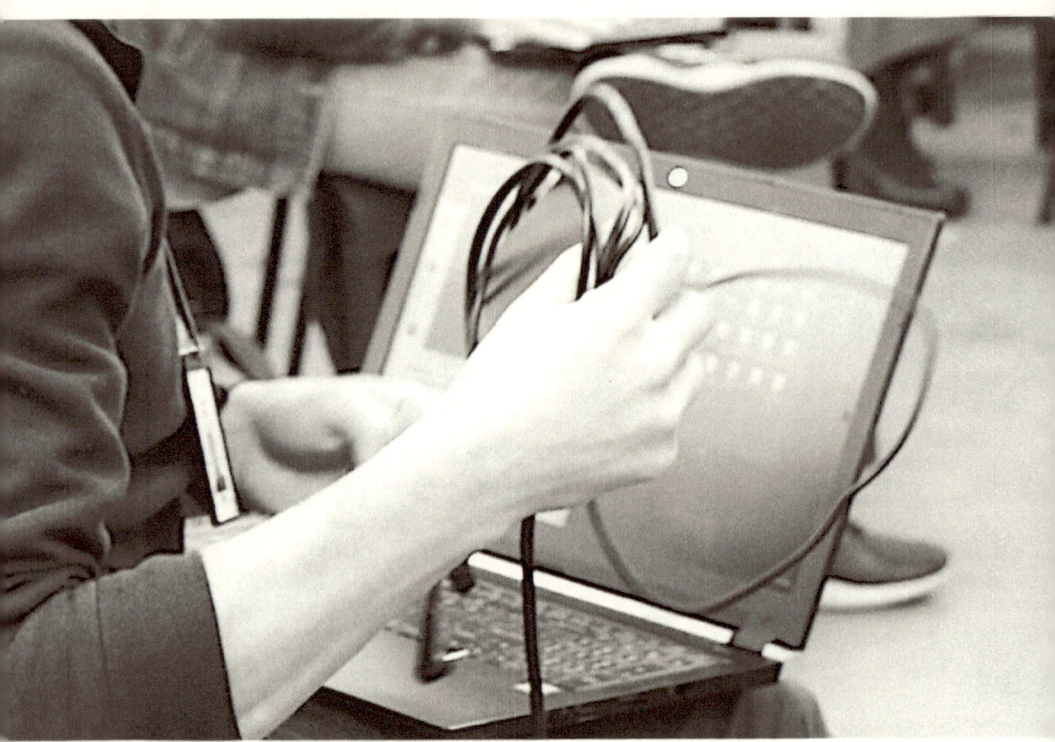

www.ingramcontent.com/pod-product-compliance
Lightning Source LLC
Chambersburg PA
CBHW021818170526
45157CB00007B/2635